FUNNY OLD WORLD

compiled by Victor Lewis-Smith

ILLUSTRATED BY
PHILIP THOMPSON

PRIVATE EYE · CORGI

Published in Great Britain
by Private Eye Productions Ltd
6 Carlisle Street, London W1V 5RG
in association with Corgi Books

ISBN 0 552 14522 X

Designed by Bridget Tisdall
Printed in England by
Ebenezer Baylis & Son Ltd, Worcester

Corgi Books are published by Transworld Publishers Ltd
61–63 Uxbridge Road, Ealing, London W5 5SA
in Australia by Transworld Publishers (Australia) Pty, Ltd
15–23 Helles Avenue, Moorebank, NSW 2170
and in New Zealand by Transworld Publishers (N.Z.) Ltd
3 William Pickering Drive, Albany, Auckland

2 4 6 8 10 9 7 5 3 1

INTRODUCTION

I think it was the late Mrs Thatcher (I am assuming that this book will stay in print for many years, and I don't want to have to keep updating it) who once said to me "you know Vic, it's a funny old world". In reply, I remarked that I was unable to concur or demur with her proposition, since I had no knowledge of any other worlds with which to compare this one, but by that point she had already moved on and was deep in conversation with the late Myra Hindley. It was that sort of a party.

What is decidedly funny is what some readers *think* is funny. It never ceases to astound me that, in every fortnight's batch of press clippings from around the planet, there's always one about a man being crushed to death by a lorry or decapitated by a circular saw, with an accompanying note reading "I was tickled by this — hope you think it's funny". These I unfailingly file in a special round filing cabinet in the corner of my room — the one with *Rubbish* written on it.

However, I never reject any clipping which touches on sexual freakishness, abnormal bodily functions, or lavatory humour. Indeed, much of this compilation is a homage to Scatologia, a celebration of the fact that some of us can still find pleasure in bum-bum and wee-wee jokes, even though we're heading for middle age. But there are also plenty of stories of human frailty, vanity, delusion, and common or garden bad luck, because (like a celebrated Antipodean transvestite) God has given me a rare and precious gift: the ability to laugh at the misfortune of others.

For those who, like me, find human futility, infirmity, deformity, and perversity endlessly fascinating, this book is (I hope) for you.

Victor Lewis-Smith
July 1996.

"THE WISE MEN say — 'If you must drink, do not drive'," Uncle Douglas told readers of the Gweru Times. "But I say, if you drink you must eat every day or not at all, otherwise you will drive yourself only to the mortuary."

Writing in his regular advice column in the paper, he continued: "A certain heavy drinker in Harare shunned all food in favour of beer, until his friends became alarmed for him. So one day, when he came to the bar, they held him on the ground and forced much sausage and millet down his throat, out of concern for his health. But, oh the spirits of the sky, a few days later, a loud explosion was heard coming from the man's toilet function area making a crack louder even than the wrathful snapping bill of the pelican.

"The concerned friends who gave him sausage and millet rushed him hurriedly to hospital but it was too late, and he died in terrible pain. A post-mortem showed that his intestines had shrunk until they only allowed liquids through. When the sausage and millet was forced down his throat, the intestines had swollen and burst. What a poor way of dying. Strange but true. Remember, all that Uncle Douglas tells you is true."

Gweru Times [Zimbabwe].

"I AM KNOWN LOCALLY as a person of sober and respectable habits," a Totnes man told reporters, "and, although I have no idea what the meaning of all this is, I suspect it has sexual overtones. I am disgusted."

The man, who lives in Seymour Court, Bridgetown, but wishes to remain anonymous, has been plagued for almost six months by a mystery caller who stuffs ties through his letterbox during the night. "The envelopes are addressed in what I can only call a brutish hand and, albeit that the ties are made by top London fashion designers, they are nevertheless extremely loud and vulgar. I am not one who deserves to have such foul ties launched at him willy-nilly, and I am thinking of donating them to charity.

"But in the meantime, make no mistake. I am regularly on sentry duty behind my letterbox with a carving knife and, if I catch this malefactor in the act, woe betide him. I'll have his fingers off in a jiffy."

The Totnes Times.

"THIS GREY-HAIRED old lady may look like a sweet little granny," counsel for the prosecution Kurt Nielsen reminded a court in Roedovre, Copenhagen, "but she faces over a hundred counts of obtaining money by deception and threats, and the state demands a custodial sentence."

Nielsen had earlier told the court how 85-year-old Tove Jensen operated her deception. "From 1988 until her arrest, she regularly invited young men to her home via a telephone message system. She claimed to be 'Marianne, a 34-year-old sex-hungry air hostess, ready for anything to satisfy your desires'. She doesn't sound like a young woman, so she told prospective clients that her voice was quaky because she was 'hot and ready for it' and asked them to come at night. When a would-be client arrived, she hid behind a window and ordered him to undress in front of an illuminated white sheet in the garden, in profile so she could 'judge him on his merits'.

"Once he was naked, she would storm into the garden dressed in a nurse's uniform (along with her adopted son, who posed as a male nurse), demand to know what on earth was going on, ask 'don't you know there's a 92-year-old woman dying in this house?', and threaten to call the police unless the naked man paid a $75 fine and left. Almost all of them paid up."

Mrs Jensen was given a suspended prison sentence, on condition she had her telephone confiscated.

The Times [Gweru, Zimbabwe].

■ **"THE SITUATION is absolutely under control," Transport Minister Ephraem Magagula told the Swaziland parliament in Mbabane. "Our nation's merchant navy is perfectly safe. We just don't know where it is, that's all."**

Replying to an MP's question, Minister Magagula admitted that the landlocked country had completely lost track of its only ship, the Swazimar: "We believe it is in a sea somewhere. At one time, we sent a team of men to look for it, but there was a problem with drink and they failed to find it, and so, technically, yes, we've lost it a bit. But I categorically reject all suggestions of incompetence on the part of this government. The Swazimar is a big ship painted in the sort of nice bright colours you can see at night. Mark my words, it will turn up. The right honourable gentleman opposite is a very naughty man, and he will laugh on the other side of his face when my ship comes in."

The Star [Johannesburg].

"When I saw the doctor, he was just as baffled as me," pensioner Maud Clarke told reporters at her home in Canterbury, Kent. "He could hardly understand my accent and kept telling the nurses that I must be from Germany, but I kept telling him my mum's a cockney from Bethnal Green and my dad's from Peckham."

Speaking with the help of an interpreter, seventy-three-year-old Maud Clarke explained what had happened to her, back in March 1994, when her voice suddenly changed beyond all recognition. "I'd just taken my neighbour Bill's dog for a walk, and got home to find my bungalow had been burgled. It was awful, and I cried so much that I lost my voice and had to be sedated. Eventually, my voice returned, but I found myself speaking in a heavy German accent, like this.

"I've had speech therapy for a year now, but it's done no good. I still speak like a German, and it gets on my nerves. Old friends phone up, hear me, think they've got the wrong number, and ring off before I can convince them I am Mrs Clarke. My grand-daughter keeps calling me Hitler, and says she wants her old granny back. Worst of all, when German tourists overhear me in shops, they start talking to me in German, and get very shirty when I can't reply to them. Funny thing is, once every few months, out of the blue, I suddenly say a sentence or two in my old London voice, and then I start being German again. And I've never been further east than Ramsgate. It makes you think, doesn't it?" *Perth Advertiser.*

"THE FIRST THING people usually notice about Feral Cheryl is that she's got pierced nipples," Leigh Duncan told a surprised audience of sales reps at a toy convention in New South Wales. "Everyone has the urge to look up a dolly's dress, and when they do they see that she's got pubic hair. They tend to get a bit of a shock.

"Feral Cheryl is the Barbie doll for alternative lifestylers. She has dreadlocks, unshaven legs, tattoos on her thighs, pierced nipples, pubic hair, vagina and clitoris, and no knickers." Ms Duncan had chosen the convention to launch her doll, named after Ferals, the extreme fringe of Australia's environmental movement who live a hunting-and-gathering existence on the east coast. "There have been written complaints, and I received some death threats because of Feral's range of accessories, including recycled tampons which can be inserted or removed, and an imitation bag of marijuana. Ferals don't relate to the clean Barbie image. Cheryl is a slut and that's that. As far as threats go, I don't give a toss. Order now, because stocks are limited."

New Zealand Sunday Star/Times.

"I HAVE SELDOM encountered the like of this in my entire career," Justice Tom Gall told the two accused men in a hushed High Court in Hong Kong. "You deliberately dumped your entire crew into the ocean, one by one, and left them to die, rather than pay them their wages."

Dismissing the appeals by Leung Kam-chuen and Kong Lai-wah against their 20-month jail sentences, Justice Gall summarised the events that took place a year earlier aboard the *Frangenti*. "When the boat approached Hong Kong, Leung asked the crew to leave their cabin one at a time and come on deck, telling them they were going to be paid. First came Tsoi Tai, 25, but, instead of paying him, Leung banged him over the head with a wooden pole, pushed him into the sea and, when he tried to climb back on board, threw live lobsters at him, forcing him back into the ocean. Then Chan Mo, 30, was asked to put on a blindfold and 'walk this way for a laugh,' and was guided overboard. Finally, Ching Sze-kan, 27, was chased all round the boat and became so terrified when Leung attempted to ram an eel up his backside that he dived into the water by himself.

Luckily, all three men were rescued by passing fishing boats, or this crime would never have been discovered.

Guilty. Appeal dismissed. You disgust me. *Eastern Express.*

● **"IT ALL HAPPENED so quickly, we can still hardly believe it," shocked worshippers told reporters outside the municipal pool in Larose, Louisiana. "Pastor Davis finished his sermon, stripped down to his bathing suit, shouted `Prepare for rebirth, ye faithful, and follow me' into his microphone, and stepped into the pool. There was a blinding flash and an almighty explosion, and next thing we saw he was floating flat on his back, dead, and the microphone had melted. It's just as well no one did follow him."**

The Larose coroners office later confirmed that Michael Davis, pastor of the Larose Christian Fellowship Church, was electrocuted as he entered the pool in which he had intended to baptise a dozen people. Faulty earthing in the microphone lead was to blame.

The Globe & Mail

"TO MY MIND, IT'S DISGUSTING. This is the third year in a row it's happened," John Holmes told ambulancemen as they carried him on a stretcher out of Bourke Central Park, New South Wales bleeding profusely and with fractures to both arms. "To my mind, kids today are completely losing sight of the true meaning of Christmas."

Speaking later from his hospital bed, Holmes explained what had happened earlier that evening: "For almost thirty years now, I've been dressing up as Santa Claus, as part of the Carols By Candlelight service in the park. I wear a red robe and a long white beard, then I drive across the park on a motorised sleigh, waving to the children and giving out sweets. To my mind, it used to be a magical event until two years ago, when a group of kids started pelting me with stones and bottles and shouting out filth. Last year to my mind, was worse, because not only did they throw things, they also urinated into the petrol tank on my sleigh, so I couldn't drive away. To my mind it's wrong that I had to call a garage truck to tow me away. It spoiled the whole effect.

But that was nothing compared to tonight. As soon as I got there, about a dozen kids, aged between eight and ten, dragged me by my beard out of my sleigh, and began kicking me in the groin, punching me in the kidneys, grabbing my sack of sweets, and trying to remove my disguise. I tried to run away, but they caught me and dragged me to the bank of the Darling river, where they partially disrobed me, broke both my arms, pissed all over me and then threw me in. Other children were crying and shouting 'don't let them hurt Santa', but their parents just stood and watched, and nobody came to help me and, to my mind, that's not on".

"To my mind, if I find out who they were, I'll kick their heads in, 10 years old or not, whatever the police say." *The Canberra Times.*

"IF I HAD MY WAY, I would ban people entirely from museums," Mr Iven M. Nzillah informed the readership of *Zambia Heritage News*. But, if they have to be allowed in, then they should wear no clothes, and it is absolutely vital that they also control their farts."

Mr Nzillah, Head of Cultural Heritage at the National Heritage Conservation Commission, went on: "Many people go to a gallery or a museum when it is raining, because it offers them the nearest shelter, but their wet clothes tend to increase humidity levels, which damages the exhibits. The humble fart, released without second thought, is just as hazardous. Research has shown that the average person produces two milligrams of sulphides a day in farts, making them the major source of pollution in a crowded gallery. The gas contains lots of acid which eats away at the silver used in old negatives and black-and-white prints.

"I agree with my colleagues in European galleries on this matter. There are only two effective solutions to the problems of damage to our national treasures. Firstly, no clothes or no admission. And secondly, people must control themselves, and cut down drastically on the amount of bio-effluent they emit. Thank you for your interest. I am going to be away from my office for two months, much against my will."

The Times of Zambia.

■ *"I HAVE promised to keep his identity confidential," said Jane Setherton, a spokesman for the Marriot Hotel, Bristol, "but I can confirm that he is no longer in our employment.*

"We asked him to clean one lift, and he spent four days on the job. When I asked him why, he replied: "Well, there are twelve of them, one on each floor, and sometimes some of them aren't there." Eventually, we realised that he thought each floor had a different lift, and he'd cleaned the same one twelve times.

"We had to let him go. It seemed best all round. I understand he is now working for Woolworths."

Bristol Evening Post.

"HE SEEMED NORMAL ENOUGH when he first arrived at the police station," a spokesman for the Montpelier gendarmerie told reporters. "He said he'd come to report the loss of a vehicle, that it was black, and that he'd mislaid the registration number. We took down the details, but started having doubts when he added that the missing vehicle had originally landed on earth 350 years ago."

The spokesman explained that the man, who had identified himself only as King Stephane Xerxes, claimed to be an extra-terrestrial from the planet Draxor, to have landed on earth in the early seventeenth century, and to have been a close friend of the composer J.S. Bach. "He said that he now had to return to his planet urgently because he'd heard that his mother was unwell, and he also had several books from Draxor public library that were overdue, and he was worried about the fine. That was why he had to find his spacecraft. Public transport is appallingly slow, he told us, whereas the craft can apparently get him to Draxor in two days. He even showed us a small piece of metal, which he said was the ignition key. We gave it to our forensic lab, who later identified it as the ring pull from a can of Coca-Cola.

"When we asked him how come he only looked about twenty-five, he went quiet for a bit. Then he told us that was because he used to sleep in his spacecraft every night, and that its rejuvenating rays kept him young. He thought that thieves had stolen his craft while he was on holiday in Antwerp last week. He's been here for three days now, and believe me, we're so sick of him that we're starting to hope that we will find his craft, just to get him off the planet."

New Straits Times, [Kuala Lumpur].

■ **"WE WERE disgusted," Ted Varey, a Belper pensioner, told reporters. "My wife's no prude, but finding two coconuts and a massive cucumber arranged in an obscene manner on our car bonnet brought on her shingles. This is the last straw. Last week there was a root vegetable rammed up the exhaust pipe also in a suggestive manner. We had to call the AA out."**

The incident was the last in a series of obscene fruit displays that have been mysteriously appearing on local cars, the work of a prowler known to the police only as "General Gherkin. "Usually it's just an apple, an orange and a banana," explained a spokesman from Mackworth College, "but now the General's started getting nasty. That last cucumber was over a foot long."

A spokesman admitted that police were baffled, but promised that all greengrocers in the Belper area would be interviewed.

The Belper Express.

"CURIOSITY? Bugger curiosity," an irate Ravishankar Raval told reporters in his home town of Jotana. "It may be a curiosity to you, but it's terrifying if you live here. Let me tell you, if it wasn't sacred, we'd slit its throat tomorrow."

Raval was complaining about the huge black goat which has menaced the inhabitants of Jotana, north Gujurat, for the past three years. "At first, it just used to sidle up to anyone with a cigarette, stand next to them and sniff their smoke. We thought it was funny to begin with, but then it started sucking the cigarettes out of their hands and smoking them itself. Not just *bidis* either, it prefers Marlboro when it can get them, and it butts us until we light one and hand it over. I've got bruises up and down my back. I reckon it's stealing about twenty a day now, all over town, and you tourists keep encouraging it. Only last week, it scared the living daylights out of a camel-cart driver. He thought it was a panther. It's getting out of control. It tried to smoke a baby's head last week, and it has to be stopped. But we're Hindus, so we can't kill it because it's holy. However, if any of you are atheists, we'd pay handsomely. I have a gun."

India Today.

"THIS REVOLTING MAN took advantage of my client's patriotism," said Prosecutor Jeanette Morrish in the Melbourne Magistrates Court. "By posing as a government agent, he persuaded her to perform hundreds of sexual favours, solely because she believed she was helping national security."

Morrish then explained how Bernie Wagner had seduced the woman (referred to in court as Miss B). "Posing as a government official, he told her that the ASIO wanted to recruit her as a secret agent. My client loves her country deeply and, while she was bemused to be given a metal-coated plastic badge with 'secret agent' on it, she accepted the offer. Wagner, a very rich man, faxed her instructions, supposedly from five other ASIO officers, and initially assigned her only to surveillance duties, for which he paid her $1,200 a month. Then, after three months, she received faxed instructions, supposedly from a senior agent, assigning her to the task of curing Agent Wagner of a terminal illness 'through the most unorthodox method — orgasm'. At first, this only involved phone sex duties, but soon she was being instructed to fly interstate to Canberra to handle the problem personally. Travel documents were provided, along with a graph plotting arousal against medical benefit. Oral sex was specified to cure palsy and grief and she was paid a $200 allowance for sexy underwear. The scam only came to light after a year, when she received a fax that, despite her efforts, Agent Wagner had died. She went to the ASIO offices in Melbourne to offer her condolences, and discovered that she wasn't an agent at all, only a dupe."

Wagner was jailed for nine months for impersonating a Commonwealth official. Miss B, after a special request, was allowed to keep her badge.

Melbourne Age.

■ **"I DO NOT KNOW what all the fuss is about," Mr Abba Bina told members of the press. "I simply placed an announcement in the local newspaper that I have resigned from the Sheriff's Office National Judicial Staff Services and am now trading as 'Mr Shit'. These are the facts of the matter. I can be located at Blackout Village, behind 4 Mile Traffic Registry. And you'd be wise to contact me, for I am Mr Shit, your specialist in chicken, cow and horse manure. Now leave me in peace."**

Papua New Guinea Postcourier.

"WHEN THE TAXI passed by, I simply thought to myself what an ugly family they all were," Officer Mustapha Garbah of the Ghanaian Motor Transport Department told a court in Accra. "It wasn't until we stopped the vehicle that we discovered the truth."

Garbah was speaking at the trial of John Ofosu, a four-foot two-inch taxi driver who had been arrested on the Accra to Kumasi road: "He was speeding, so we gave chase and ordered him to stop. While my colleague was writing out a speeding ticket, I looked again at the passenger in the front seat and suddenly realised it was not an ugly person at all, but a pregnant goat in a t-shirt. Investigating further, I found all thirteen other passengers were also pregnant goats, all in t-shirts."

Ofosu admitted fourteen specimen charges of stealing unattended animals from roadside villages in the Ashanti region. He and an accomplice, Boakye Tetteh, admitted they'd been dressing stolen goats in t-shirts for years, so as not to arouse suspicion while they drove home, and had never been apprehended before. Both were remanded in custody for sentencing.
Daily Graphic [Ghana].

“I FEEL RESPONSIBLE. The phrase ‘you cunt’ is hardly the sort of language people expect to hear on a family trip to the zoo,” confessed Jack Corney to reporters. “But it is difficult to teach a parrot control. I may well have to sack Bluey from the kiddies’ show.”

Corney, owner of the Isle of Wight Zoo, Sandown, acknowledged that his star parrot’s career was now under review. “Where he learned it from we don’t know, but the language he uses is more suited to a stag night than a family show, F-words, B-words, the lot. We’ve had no formal complaints, and it always brings the house down when he tells the female presenters to ‘show us yer tits’, but it really won’t do.

“Bluey is not as big a problem as Charlie, our Capuchin monkey, though. He rattles the bars of his cage and whoops until he’s attracted a crowd of schoolgirls, and then relieves himself. I duck every time I pass him by. It’s not nice.”
Isle of Wight County Press.

■ **FOR YEARS, well-meaning pilots have attempted to scatter cremated remains from airplanes for families, friends, or business. Now, accomplish this task efficiently with Trail’s End Cremains Scattering Dispersion Units and be assured that:**

1. **Aircraft paint will NOT be “sand blasted” from the cremated remains.**
2. **The pilot will NOT be dangerously distracted while flying.**
3. **There will be NO logistical problem getting cremains outside a moving aircraft.**
4. **There will be NO “blow back”.**
5. **There will be NO “spillage”.**

All units are handheld, and come with instructions, plastic explosives, goggles and a kit for starting your own cremains scattering business. A must for Flying Clubs.

A. **Deluxe model, fits large window** **$199.00**
B. **Small window model, fits 4in by 6in** **$399.00**

Trail’s End Cremains Scattering Service Inc, 3279 Silverthorne Drive, Ft Collins, Colorado 80526. *Private Pilot.*

"THE DEVIL MADE me do it, make no mistake about that," declared David Wylie, while defending himself in the Magistrates Court in Larne. "I'm telling you, it wasn't the real me who committed this vile act, it was my former self, before I became a born-again Christian. When a Christian goes out, he must wear his best armour to protect himself against Satan, but I wasn't wearing armour — just my pyjamas."

An RUC officer had earlier informed Magistrate Robert Alcom of the circumstances that led to 32-year-old Wylie's arrest on a charge of indecency: "On the morning in question, I went to Drumalis Convent because one of the Sisters had telephoned the station and asked us to come quickly, because the nuns had spotted a man doing 'something unspeakable' with a bicycle in the convent grounds. When I got there, I saw Mr Wylie in the cloister, his underpants round his knees, performing a bizarre sexual act with a nun's bicycle. He'd smeared lubricating cream on the saddle, and was having sexual intercourse with the seat, while simultaneously reading a pornographic magazine called Filthy Habits, which featured nuns. When I asked what he was doing, he said it was 'based on things I saw while I was working in London,' and added that 'The Devil's work is everywhere'. At that point, we arrested him."

A spokesnun for the Cross and Passion Sisters later told reporters: "It was disgusting, we were all very shocked about it. It's not the kind of thing you expect to see outside a convent window first thing in the morning. We want to put this behind us." The case was adjourned for a Probation Service report.

Sunday World [Dublin].

"THIS WAS A CLUMSY attempt by a caring and gentle person to find a first girlfriend," Mr Derek Reed told Teignbridge Magistrates. "It is plainly a bizarre incident, and my client is of strictly limited intelligence, but he never meant to cause harm or to frighten the woman involved."

Earlier, the court had heard the chain of circumstances that led Nicholas Green, 35, from Newton Abbot, to plead guilty to a charge of indecent assault. "My client, who has never had a girlfriend, has a very unusual fetish for plastic macs and clingfilm. When he first saw the woman in question, she was walking with crutches after an accident, and he offered to come to her home and make her a stool. She accepted his offer but, instead of bringing tools to her home, he brought a large post office sack full of plastic raincoats, tipped them onto the floor, asked her to pick her favourite colour, and then began dressing her in the macs. When he got to the third coat, he produced the roll of clingfilm and began to wrap her in it, thereby trapping her arms. The woman complained that this was not the proper way to construct a stool, and that she was getting hot, but he continued, putting a total of eleven plastic raincoats and three rolls of clingfilm on her while repeating: "I am Captain Polymer, your friend, and I love you."

Magistrates sentenced Green to two years probation, on condition that he also received psychiatric help.

Herald Express [South Devon].

■ **WAITING FOR TRAFFIC is sometimes a very tedious thing," said Roberto Nacianceno, addressing delegates at a meeting of the Metro Manila Development Authority. "That's why our traffic police are now being trained to entertain motorists by learning trafficgraphy — a blend of traffic and choreography."**

MMDA chairman Prospero Oreta had earlier explained how the dancing policemen would lift the spirits of Filipino motorists. "The idea originally comes from the famous dancing cops of Bangkok. But Thai policemen always dance on their own, whereas Manila's trafficgraphy uses an entire troupe of dancing policemen. Our first group, the Los Del Rios began dancing last week, and have already performed in some of the city's busiest intersections. They wear bright blue shirts and short pants, and direct traffic while dancing to the tune of 'Macarena'. It cheers up the motorists. The only problem we have had is that some drivers become so enthralled that they stop, and have to be prodded to drive on. This system is a great improvement on the loudspeakers which we tried last year. Those have now been withdrawn, because officials kept using them to hurl insults and obscenities at anyone who didn't obey the traffic signals."
The China Post.

NORMAN KEITH Hireme, a worker at the Tegel Poultry Plant who used a chicken as an offensive weapon, was fined $50 after being found guilty of cruelty.

"Mr Hireme took a live chicken, pointed the bird's rear at fellow workers, and squeezed it with such force that excrement shot several metres and struck a colleague in the face," RSPCA worker Jim Boyd told a New Plymouth District Court. "He repeated this several times before replacing it on the conveyor belt, where it was electrically stunned and slaughtered a few seconds later. Considerable force has to be used to fire excrement such a great distance. Never mind about the employees, it must have been most unpleasant for the chicken."
Wellington Evening Post.

■ **"WIND FUCKER.** An obsolete term, known from a single record of 1599 'The kistrilles or windfuckers that fill themselves with winde, fly against the winde euermore' (OED). It may be compared with another kestrel name Fuckwind, given as a northern term by Halliwell 1847. The OED also records the present word as an expression of opprobrium in sources from the early years of the 17th century, eg 1609: 'Did you euer heare such a Wind-Fucker as this?' To interpret the names Wind Fucker and Fuckwind, we need to establish if *fuck*, attested since 1503, could once have had another meaning. We notice the cognate Dutch *fokken* to fuck, also to knock, the German *ficken* to fuck, in dialect to beat. Taking the sense of knock, beat to be more original, and assuming the same for English, we at once have an explanation of the bird names: they are literally wind beater and beatwind, in allusion to the beating wings of the hovering bird, as in the synonym WIND FANNER. The present bird names thus uniquely preserve fuck in its hitherto unrecognised, primary sense."

The Oxford Book of British Bird Names.

"FIRM BUT FAIR is my motto," Officer Boniface Onyeabor told a Coroner's Court in Anambra state. "The man was a thief, and he deserved all he got."

Onyeabor, of the Anambra State Police, was giving evidence at an inquest into the death of Tfawa Ojukwu in Enugu. "Ojukwu was a notorious genitals thief. He would go up to people, shake hands with them, and moments later they would discover that their testicles had been stolen. Luckily, that night, one of his victims raised the alarm and a crowd chased after Ojukwu, cornering him in National Square, shouting 'genitals thief' at him, beating him up, and setting him alight with a tyre necklace.

"By the time I arrived in the square, Ojukwu was already ablaze. It was far too late to save him, so I waited until the flames died down, and then ordered a passing driver to take the remains to the mortuary. The driver refused, calling me 'naughty policeman' and implying that I had buggered my mother. So I shot him. Then I ordered another driver to take both bodies away. There was no more trouble. As I said, firm but fair. That is my motto.

"When it was all over, the victim thanked me, and told me that he had got his testicles back again. Kind words like that make my job seem worthwhile."

Khaleej Times.

■ **"DEAR SIR, This year is the five-year anniversary of the death of my friend, gay playwright Robert Chesley. I and another of Robert's good friends would like to get together with other people who knew and loved him to schmooze, celebrate, and listen to some sexual readings — things that Robert would have appreciated.**

If you knew Robert, had sex with Robert, acted in one of his plays, jerked off in the Y steam room with Robert, attended one of his velching parties or was just on the receiving end of his famous verbal abuse, please come and join us on Thursday December 21, at 7:30. We have slides taken of him in a Bangkok club which are touching and erotic. And probably illegal. Mark J. Chester. San Francisco."

San Francisco Bay Guardian.

SEVEN WOMEN SHALL TAKE HOLD OF ONE MAN IN THAT DAY... ISAIAH 4:1.

Isaiah 4:1 is a prophecy of seven women going and marrying one man. Hereby note that I, Cyril Gobbley, am willing to be that man, and so fulfill Scripture. If you are a nubile sweety and desire to be one of my seven brides so that you too can help fulfill Scripture, then send a photograph to Box 7134 Saskatoon, SK, Canada, S7K 4J1. My intentions are (all) most honourable. We're doing it because we love the Lord."

The Star Phoenix.

"I WANT THE MONEY. ***I will not accept anything less than $200,000 for them," Sridhar Chillal told reporters gathered outside his house in Pune, India. "People pay through the ears for an extinct butterfly or a rare stamp. But these are more special. These are the only fingernails of their kind in the world. I want the money. A museum will give me the money. God has told me."***

Chillal, 59, was hoping to find a buyer for his fingernails. "They are the world's longest fingernails. My left hand nails total 226 inches, with a 52-inch thumbnail. I began growing them at school, 45 years ago, after breaking by mistake a long nail grown by my teacher. He challenged me to grow nails as long as his, that is how I started. It took me seven years to get married, because no girl wanted anything to do with these nails. Eventually, I married a close relative with a hare lip. My job as a photographer was also very hard, because I have to keep my nails in this special black pouch and it is hard to operate a camera with one hand. Because of my nails, I have become famous throughout India, but now they are causing problems. I cannot do what other men can with their hands. I do not sleep properly, I have a 24-hour headache, the blood circulation to my brain has been greatly affected, I cannot hear properly, and there are pains in the tips of my left fingers. Typing is out of the question. So, as long as the price is right, I feel it is time for a change."

The Jeddah News.

"When I told them I'd sold out of sleeping pills, the pensioners turned very vicious," pharmacist S.Y. Yue told a public enquiry in Jiangsu. "I couldn't understand it. They kept shouting that they must beat the deadline somehow, and that they needed the pills for an overdose. Then they head-butted my drug cabinet and rushed into the street, where they threw themselves in front of a passing lorry."

The enquiry was investigating the suicides of more than a hundred elderly people in Haian county, Jiangsu, after a government decree, issued on March 15, announced that cremation would be compulsory for anyone dying after April 1st. "Many old people believe that, if they are not buried, their ancestors will be insulted," said a government official, "so, during that fortnight, they were killing themselves in any way they could think of. Sleeping pills were most popular, but others were throwing themselves off bridges, drowning themselves in rivers, or hanging themselves. One old man who tried to gas himself caused a house fire, so he ended up being cremated anyway."

South China Morning Post.

● **"IT'S NOT EVERY DAY you see a scrotum that size," recalled William A. Morton, a retired Pennsylvanian urologist. "It was twice the size of a melon, black and blue, and it stank. The patient told me that he'd injured himself a month earlier in the machine shop where he worked. I nearly passed out when he told me he 'knew enough about doctoring to close the wound with a heavy-duty stapling gun'. Later, I removed eight rusty one-inch staples from the scrotum, and reconnected the stump of his spermatic cord, although the left testis was missing.**

"After the operation, the patient broke down and confessed what had really happened. Apparently, he used to masturbate in his lunch hour by holding his penis against the canvas drive-belt of a machine, but had lost concentration one day and leaned too close to the belt. His scrotum had been caught between the pulley and the drive belt, and he ended up being thrown right across the workshop and straight through a window. Too stunned to realise that he had lost a testicle, he stapled up the wound and resumed work.

"He assured me that he would abandon this method of self-gratification from now on, and buy a sex doll. Sorry, but I think he needs psychiatric help."

Medical Aspects of Human Sexuality.

● **"I LEFT THE *Heavenly Dog Sect* in 1992 after sustaining head injuries, due to an accident involving local militant butchers," Chen Qi-zan declared to Helen Sze during a recent interview. "I realised then that self-awareness could only be attained by focusing one's mind on the penis. This made me realise it was stupid to worship dogs, so I founded the *Penis Worship Sect*."**

Standing on one leg, Chen outlined the doctrine of his religion, which has so far met with widespread derision in Taipei. "Men have two minds, one in their heads and one in their genitals. The woman's penis is in the breasts, which have enough strength to lift 1,000kg if harnessed properly. The male penis can lift loads of up to 500kg. I am now practising a feat called *The King's Wonder Power*, for which I have to train my penis for at least six hours a day. It is the kind of feat that should only be attempted by people with strong minds, because you will lose your balance and harmony if you try this before you are ready. When you reach the highest level, the penis can walk, talk, even sing on its own. It will tell you your fortune. I have had two winning lottery tickets during the past year, after following the guidance of my divine penis."

After a pause, Chen continued: "There are few people who have the courage to declare in public that they worship penises. My friends, do not be afraid. In the future, those who harness this power will rule the world."
Eastweek [Hong Kong].

"SHAU KEI WAN is extremely guilty of something," Superintendent Ray Pierce of the Hong Kong police force told reporters. "He must be. We're just not sure exactly what it is though, so we've released him on bail until we can decide what to charge him with."

Superintendent Pierce, the Mong Kok police assistant district commander for crime, was giving details about the arrest of Shau Kei Wan, 34, a factory worker who had earlier been detained in the Grand Tower shopping centre. "He's a peeping tom with some kind of underwear fetish, and he's admitted that his favourite pastime is to follow women in mini skirts. He has a palmcorder hidden inside a black box, along with a torch and zoom lens, all on the end of a long control stick. He gets behind the women as they step onto the shopping mall escalators, positions his palmcorder between their legs pointing upwards, and then pushes the record button. Usually, the women have no idea that anything's going on, only on this occasion Wan pressed the playback button by mistake, and the victim got a blast of an old pop video up her skirt. She screamed, there was a struggle as he tried to get his equipment back, and the security guards arrested him. We found a dozen videotapes when we raided his house, with footage of over a hundred pairs of women's knickers on them. If that's not a crime, then I don't know what is. Only trouble is, he doesn't actually seem to have broken any law."

Eastern Express

"PUT IT THIS WAY," prosecuting counsel told Richmond Magistrates Court, "if Jonathan Meades had been reviewing Arthur's Bistro that evening, the place would have been out of business within a week."

Wheelchair-bound pensioner Peter Grier, 78, of Twickenham, was accused of indecent exposure, threatening behaviour, being drunk and disorderly, and assaulting a policeman after an incident at the bistro in Twickenham Green. The prosecution continued: "Wheeling his way to the bistro, which he alleged was conspiring against him, Grier exposed his penis to members of the staff, causing a waitress to flee in some distress. He then removed his colostomy bag, which was full to overflowing, and hurled it at the window, smearing the glass and spreading its contents over several tables and chairs, while shouting: 'This used to be a public karzee' at bemused diners, until he was arrested.

"It is true that the restaurant is a converted public toilet, and Mr Grier has been waging a one-man campaign against the building's change of purpose. He was banned from the premises after an unsavoury incident in January involving a saveloy, but, on 24 March, he went berserk with his colostomy bag after spending all day on the Green, sitting in his wheelchair and drinking a mixture of creme de menthe and a medicine known as 'Night Nurse'."

The court later heard that Grier had a history of colostomy terrorism, including incidents outside an off-licence and an estate agents earlier in the year. At this point, Grier interrupted with shouts of "I can take my drink, I was in the Navy" and, after being cautioned by magistrates, was wheeled out by an usher.

Richmond & Twickenham Times.

● **"I AM A RUSSIAN lady now for visit to Bangkok three weeks. But I not for coming odalisque or twirling trull. Also I not use phone for meeting short friend for money. But I am liking very much idea of inferior Minister Chavalit saying to keep all open until 3.00am. Darling idea and darling man. I think he faithful in his resting holes, and not such a man of anxious glands. God bless him and never to heal up his cracks."**

(Letter to the Editor from Miss Olga Pushanov, in response to attempts by Thailand's Interior Minister, Chavalit Yongchaiyudh, to keep bars in Bangkok's red light district open until 3am.) *The Nation.*

"DONKEY SANCTUARIES? Piss and wind to donkey sanctuaries!" screamed Mr Venkatachalapathy, chairman of the Thanjavur municipal council. "I tell you, a whack up the bottom is the only language these animals understand."

Chairman Venkatachalapathy was addressing a council meeting, hastily convened after several townspeople complained of assaults by stray donkeys: "One of these cursed animals ran amok only this afternoon, attacking anyone wearing black. It wandered into the magistrates' court campus, bit a municipal clerk in a black jacket, and then severely attacked a young man in black pants. A magistrate, passing by in his black gown, was chased across campus and only avoided injury by climbing a drainpipe and hanging there for over an hour, an indignity scarcely befitting his rank. Luckily, a quick-thinking group of men saw his plight, chased the donkey with clubs, and wisely whacked it up the bottom until it ran away. That is the fate that all stray donkeys should meet, and I implore the council to pass my resolution to that effect."

Asked whether it wasn't more usual for red clothes to anger animals, Chairman Venkatachalapathy replied: "We have an answer to that. We think this donkey was colour-blind." His motion was narrowly defeated.

The Times of India News Service.

"IT WAS THE FILTHY, foul-mouthed verbal assaults more than the actual violence that really upset my son," Martha Shear told reporters. "It's not right that my seven-year-old should hear the Mighty Mouse, his favourite animal character, shouting at him: 'I'm going to kick the fucking crap out of you, you little bastard'."

Mrs Shear described the incident which occurred outside the Chuck E. Cheese pizza parlour. "I invited my son's friends there for his birthday party, because Chuck E. Cheese — the Mighty Mouse — usually puts on such a good show for the children on the lawn outside. Michael's at that curious age, so he sneaked up on Chuck during the show and yanked the head off his costume. It was naughty, but didn't merit what happened next. The old guy inside the costume grabbed my son, said he'd had enough of crap like him, threw him onto a wooden bench, and started kicking the living daylights out of him in front of the other kids. I screamed at Chuck to stop, but he just kept jumping up and down on my boy. In the end, it took four short order chefs to pull him off, and now Michael's in hospital with concussion. After all that, the guy went into his fire-eating routine and tried to set himself alight."

Washington Post.

■ ***"THIS IS NOT JUST A MORAL ISSUE," declared a spokesman from the vice squad of Xiangzhou city police. "More seriously, these people are clearly contravening the terms of their pension by continuing to work."***

He was speaking shortly after police had jailed the members of two prostitution rings operating in the city's central Fengboshan Park. "I've never seen anything like it. The oldest was 93. The madam told us her 'girls' — all aged over 70 — catered for 200 clients a month, and offered a wide range of services. Nude peeking was 5 yuan, bosom-touching was 10 yuan, manual relaxation was 50 yuan and oral relief was 60 yuan, rising to 80 yuan if the client wanted the teeth out.

"We recognised that the park is in the Zhuhai Special Enterprise Zone, where private businesses are strongly encouraged but, even so, such conduct is quite unacceptable." *South China Morning Post.*

"We currently have fifty-four prisoners on Death Row and the number is going up every week," complained Vicente Vinarao in a letter to Senator Ernesto Herrara. "Frankly, we've got no idea what to do with them at the moment. Except wait for them to die of old age, I suppose."

Vinarao, the Director of the Bureau of Corrections, was complaining to the Parliament of the Philippines of the unforeseen consequences of a law it had passed last year, reviving capital punishment. "At present, we are at a total loss as to how to carry out the wishes of parliament, because the Philippines still has no electric chair or gas chamber. The law specifies electrocution as the only permitted method of execution until a gas chamber can be built, but a bolt of lightning destroyed the country's only electric chair several years ago, and the Bureau doesn't have the six million pesos ($330,460) needed to buy a new one. As for building a gas chamber, work on that was halted by the safety inspector in April after the brickwork was found to be leaking gas. He said the building might be injurious to public health."
The Straits Times.

"THERE'S NO DOUBT about it, it was another case of likhubalo," Inspector Mdluli of the Simunye police force informed reporters. "They looked like a three-headed octopus. I have never seen anything like it."

He explained what he had discovered after being called to a house in Lusoti on Monday morning. "The unnamed threesome were locked together in coitus, and unable to move. The woman confessed to me that, when her husband had gone away on business on Friday, she had invited her lover and his friend into the house. But, after simultaneous vaginal and anal penetration, they found themselves locked together in what is called a *double dog's knot*, with both men quite unable to withdraw. For three days they lay there helplessly, until a neighbour heard their cries for help and entered the room. She laughed so much it took her an hour to collect herself and phone for help. I immediately realised the husband must have been to a witch doctor and given likhubalo root to his wife. Men often do this if they think their wives are unfaithful, and it's very effective, because any man other than her husband gets stuck fast.

"When the husband returned, he eventually agreed to release the two men in the traditional way, by making them all beg for mercy, ritually forgiving them, and then showing his wife a padlock and key. When the padlock opened up, so did she. It's basic science, really."

The Times of Swaziland.

"The accused is obviously a perfectly normal and sane individual" Justice Nicholson told the High Court in Belfast, "who happened to go berserk for several months because of the onion incident. I am therefore releasing him on bail."

Alfred Weeks, a landscape gardener from Lisburn, was accused of arson, burglary and bomb hoaxes. A Crown lawyer alleged that "Mr Weeks ordered a cheeseburger without onions from Julie's Kitchen, but the staff there put onions in it. Mr Weeks didn't want onions, and felt humiliated in front of his friends, so over the next few months he took his revenge. First, he daubed 'They give you onions when you don't want them in this dump' over their windows at night. Then he broke in and smashed their drinks dispenser and cash register. During opening hours, he fired ball bearings through their windows. A bomb hoax followed — the army had to carry out a controlled explosion — and finally he broke into the restaurant and set fire to it, causing £16,000 worth of damage."

Outside, Mr Weeks told reporters: "I've promised not to do it again, and I've written a letter of apology to the staff, those that are left anyway. Looking back, it's hard to say now why I got so upset. It's not that I hate onions. I just will not stand for sloppy service and impertinence from shop girls." *Irish News.*

■ "WHAT THE PROSECUTION says is technically true," lawyer Henri Janssens admitted to a court in Brasschaat, Belgium. "Before prescribing contact lenses, my client, who is a state registered optician, did indeed frequently order women to strip naked and dance around his consulting room while he played the accordian. However, there are mitigating circumstances which I ask the magistrates to take into consideration. The fact is that the defendant qualified in England where, he assures me, such techniques are commonplace."

The defendant was later acquitted.

Portsmouth Journal Series.

● *"FRESH SALIVA IS NOW our store's number one seller," Shukan Isomura of the Wakayama company told a trade conference in Takarazuka City. "No sooner do we put the bottles onto the shelves than they are sold out, and our only fear is that supplies may dry up."*

Fresh saliva is the latest specialist product to be marketed by the Wakayama company, aimed at Japanese men with an obsessive interest in joshikosei *(female high school students). "Last year we began selling* joshikosei *used panties in our stores, and sales are so good that we've invested in vending machines for them. But fresh saliva from joshikosei is proving to be even more popular. For 3,000 yen, customers get a 50ml bottle with a photograph of the donor on the label, and our Tokyo store is selling 300 units a week. Freshness is all, so we keep it refrigerated and guarantee that it's no more than seven days old. It's now easier for the girls to sell their saliva than their panties and, if we can get regular supplies, we're planning to start bottling* joshikosei *menstrual fluid next year." Mainichi Daily News [Japan].*

"I SHOULD HAVE listened to an old man's wisdom," Mzee Opesen declared to members of the Ugandan Ongino Christian Youth. "My grandfather told me: 'Always wear underpants beneath your kanzu before you mount your bicycle'. Foolishly I mocked him, and now my heart is a dry ear pod."

Opesen explained to the youths what had happened. "I was cycling home from the market, dressed only in my spotless white kanzu, when a terrible whirlwind appeared. It blew up my kanzu, ballooning it over my face and lifting me far above the ground. I kept control but, when the bike landed, I sat down hard upon my own testicles, squashing them against the saddle to the flatness of patties. A sharp pain ran through my entire body. Then I felt a deep inner peace and I went into a deep sleep."

Opesen was taken to the dispensary, and regained consciousness an hour later. "All my life I have tried to maintain the proud ancient dress of those olden days of Semei Kakungulu," he said sadly, "but no longer. I am deformed and shall cloak my manhood in trousers." Two youths fainted during the speech and received medical attention.
The Monitor [Kampala].

■ "I AM A SAINTLY MAN. Things are never what they seem," protested Thai monk Samai Parnthong to a Bangkok court. "It was dark and she did not resist my advances. I did not know she had been dead for three days."

Parnthong, who has since been expelled from his monastery, admitted to committing a variety of sexual acts with a corpse. Bum Wo, prosecuting counsel, told the judge: "The dead woman's relatives were midway through the third night of mourning and prayer in the Rassadorn Pathong temple when they heard sounds of splitting wood. Discovering Parnthong on top of the corpse, they began beating him senseless while shouting: 'He is damaging the coffin, kill him, kill him'. His life was only saved the police, who placed him under arrest."

Parnthong was fined 500 baht for creating a public nuisance while drunk, and given two years in prison for damaging the coffin. Necrophilia is not an offence in Thailand.
The Nation [Indonesia].

● *"IN LHASA, I wanted to use a typical public toilet, so I went to one near the Holiday Inn. A small child directed me, intentionally I believe, to the wrong entrance, the one from where the shit is collected. I should have realised this, of course, because of his uncontrollable giggling.*

"What looked to me like a brown floor turned out to be a swimming pool full of shit. I took one little step and fell in. It was really deep and I went under, swallowed several mouthfuls, and then managed to get out, completely covered in shit. I had to walk back to the Holiday Inn because I wasn't allowed on the bus, but when I walked in the staff threw me out complaining that I was covered in shit. A group of Italians outside the hotel tried to hose me down on the lawn next door. I took my clothes off and the water was extremely cold, which they thought very amusing. Eventually a very nice man smoking a pipe from the Holiday Inn sent somebody to take me inside. I felt quite embarrassed as I walked through the lobby, naked and still covered in shit.

"I went to the doctor because I was concerned that swallowing shit may not be good for your health. He gave me some medicine for worms. I had to throw away my backpack, and my money went a funny colour and stank of shit for a few days, so I had trouble spending it. Neither my passport nor student card looked very nice. I am currently trying to get new ones. I read in the Lonely Planet Guide that no one has ever fallen into a Tibetan toilet. Please correct that statement in future editions.

"Kerstin Knopf – Germany."

Letter in Planet Talk [Lonely Planet Quarterly Newsletter].

"I KNOW THINGS probably look bad for me," Joel Okitel told officers from the Kampala police force, as they arrested him on a charge of manslaughter. "But when you have heard the full story, I am sure that you will let me walk free."

Okitel explained the circumstances that had led to the killing at his house in Mornita village in Nyero, Kumi district. "For some years, it has been my practice to keep 100,000 shillings in banknotes in a sock inside my pillow, but yesterday I found the bundle was gone. My underpants were also missing, and I suspected that my wife, Mary Asio, who is a slut, had given them to a witch doctor to make me impotent and had stolen the money to pay him. When I accused her, she denied everything and attempted to bite off my genitals. I shouted 'slut, slut!' and lashed out at her with a stick. This upset a millet steamer which, unfortunately, toppled over, killing our six-month-old baby instantly. Next day, while digging the baby's grave, I found the money and underpants, along with some socks and my wife's half-petty and brassieres, all hidden in a rat's nest. The rat was clearly a criminal so I killed it, Mary roasted it, and we both feasted. I tell you, I am innocent."

New Vision [Kampala].

● **"GOLDIE'S always liked playing 'fetch' with sticks, so I guess this was second nature to him," Ross White told journalists outside his Melbourne home.**

White was talking to reporters about his cross-bred terrier, whose left hind leg had been severed the night before by a passing train. "He must have been a bit shaken, but he picked the leg up in his mouth, hopped two kilometres home with it, barked once, dropped the leg, and collapsed in the doorway. The vet tried sewing it back on, but frankly, he made a balls of it. I assume the man was drunk. He sewed it onto his stomach. Even I know that's not where a dog's leg should go. It fell off this morning, and I'm not paying his bill. Still, Goldie's doing okay. We're thinking of changing his name to 'Tripod'."

The Melbourne Age.

"SO ANYWAY, I opened the soup can and found soup inside," Tom Cummins told reporters outside his home in Austin, Texas. "Soup. Then it dawned on me. My life is in ruins, and I don't mean I'm an archaeologist. I mean, I'm a dead man. Give to charity? Stuff it. Never again. One good deed and I'm over $70,000 out of pocket."

Cummins, a colour film processor at a local electronics company, explained what had happened to him a week earlier. "I was watching TV just before Christmas, and they were talking about a charity food drive, collecting canned food to give to homeless people. My wife Trixie and I cried as we watched. We'd had a few drinks and immediately started gathering most of the tins we had in the kitchen, drove them down to the depot, and handed them over. I'd forgotten all about it until yesterday, when we were getting ready for a toga party and Trixie asked me to get her diamond necklace. So I picked up the fake Campbell's soup can where we keep our valuables and tried to open it. I couldn't twist the top off, but at first I just thought it was rusty, so I used a can opener to open the lid. But inside there was only Scotch Broth. I remember saying to Trixie 'I don't feel too good,' just before I passed out. I phoned the police, but they said there's nothing they can do, because no crime had been committed and warned me that using foul language over the phone was an offence. They then charged me for spraying the legend 'robbing cheating scum' over the windows of the insurance company. They won't pay up, because they say I threw the jewels away myself. And my Trixie has left me to start a new life running a cattery in Dallas. I don't know where she got the cash from."

Police later confirmed that they wish to interview a homeless Austin man in his sixties who recently received a food parcel and was last heard of booking a flight to the Bahamas.
Austin Herald.

"KITE FLIERS demand justice," chanted Rodney Hope, in a lone protest outside the Fontabelle offices of the *Barbados Advocate*. "Editor, obey the rules. Fascism begins this way."

Brandishing a placard bearing the slogan ADVOCATE SMALL KITE SHAM, Hope, from Eden Lodge, St Michael, demanded a public inquiry into the judging of the newspaper's annual small kite competition: "It's an outrage. It's a small kite competition and my 2cm kite was the smallest, but the judges gave the prize to a 6in kite and then said there'd been a mix-up with names. The same thing happened last year, too. They announced me as the winner, but then gave the $200 dollar prize to someone else with a 9in kite, and said there'd been a mix-up. Mix-up my posterior. It's favouritism."

Commenting on the situation, the *Advocate's* Vice-President for Marketing and Sales, Mr Tony Cumberbatch, said: "It's true that this is a small kite competition, and Mr Hope's entry was by far the smallest, but there's more to it than that. He claimed that his 2cm kite could fly but, when we investigated, he was obviously holding it on a piece of stiff wire, and not on string. When we tied a piece of thread onto it, and asked him to try again, he couldn't get it up, and it fell to earth like a stone. In our opinion, if it don't fly it ain't a kite. He was also squeezing a rubber ball in his left trouser pocket. I cannot be certain this was anything to do with cheating, but I didn't like it. The judges' decision is final, thank you."

The Barbados Advocate.

● "IT IS WELL-KNOWN THAT the kneecaps of the dead have magical properties," a police spokesman told reporters in the central Philippine town of Bacolod, where residents had been complaining about nocturnal hammering sounds from a nearby cemetery. "We have discovered that a gang of voodoo fanatics has been raiding dozens of tombs in recent weeks, unearthing the bodies and stealing only the knees. These wicked thieves pound the kneecaps into powder, which they then burn like incense outside any house which they want to rob. The smoke from the kneecaps puts the occupants to sleep, and the thieves can then burgle the house. Until these criminals are caught, undertakers will therefore be removing kneecaps from all corpses before burial." *Trinidad Guardian.*

"WE WILL NOT have him put down. Lucky is basically a damn good guide dog," Ernst Gerber, a dog trainer from Wuppertal told reporters. "He just needs a little brush-up on some elementary skills, that's all."

Gerber admitted to the press conference that Lucky, a German shepherd guide-dog for the blind, had so far been responsible for the deaths of all four of his previous owners. "I admit it's not an impressive record on paper. He led his first owner in front of a moving bus, and the second off the end of a pier. He actually pushed the third owner off a railway platform just as the Cologne to Frankfurt express was approaching, and he walked his fourth owner into heavy traffic, before abandoning him and running away to safety. But, apart from the epileptic fits, he has a lovely temperament. And guide dogs are difficult to train these days."

Asked if Lucky's fifth owner would be told about his previous record, Gerber replied: "No. It would make them nervous, and that would make Lucky nervous. And when Lucky gets nervous, he's liable to do something silly." *Europa Times.*

"JOYCE WAS ONE of Oxford's great characters," former Police Superintendent Ted East told reporters. "I always remember him coming up to me in the street and shouting, 'That's the policeman who likes dressing up in drag'. That's the kind of man he was."

East was amongst those paying tribute to Thomas John Joyce, Oxford's oldest and most celebrated transvestite, whose death had just been announced. Shopkeeper Ray Murphy recalled: "Joyce used to be a bus conductor, and became famous after he got sacked for performing the dance of the seven veils in the staff canteen. After that he got really outlandish. He took to drink, dyed his hair yellow, started wearing chiffon, and used to claim 'I'm the queen of Oxford and I don't care who knows it'. When he was over sixty, he held up the buses in Cornmarket Street, dressed as Marilyn Monroe, and frequently got arrested for taking all his clothes off in the city centre. He told magistrates he was scratching an itching pile, but they fined him £10 anyway. Another time, he dressed up in blue nylons and high heels and wrote 'nigger lover' on the back of the bus of a driver he didn't like. They fined him £10 for that too."

Oxford solicitor John Simms added: "Joyce would turn up to court in fish-net tights, with a chiffon scarf and pink top. I remember him putting on his make-up in the reflection of the court noticeboard glass. Once he was in court though, he was actually quite respectful. We shall miss him."

The Oxford Times.

■ **"THIS IS AN outrage," screamed Pathumrat Piaklin outside the Appeal Court in Chiang Mai, as a convicted murderer walked free. "Dwarf or giant, we are all equal in stature under the law."**

Piaklin was leading a delegation of midgets protesting against the freeing of Richard David Walker, an Australian convicted of killing Hong Katonk Chamnong, a dwarf: "Hong and I were bouncers at the Sunshine nightclub. On the night of Hong's death, Walker was drunk and abusive, so we decided to throw him out. Usually, people think being bounced by midgets is funny and they go quietly, but Walker began arguing, said he'd been over-charged for drinks, and kneed Hong in the face. We got angry, and each grabbed one of Walker's legs and clung on, trying to drag him out of the club. But Walker shook me free, and then trod on Hong several times, crushing him with his foot. It was dreadful."

Giving the appeal court ruling, Judge Amnawong said: "Chamnong was less than 90cm tall, and persons of such restricted growth are easily killed by accident. It happens all the time. Walker has apologised, said he didn't mean to kill anyone, and paid 200,000 baht to Chamnong's family. He could hardly have been more considerate. Conviction overturned. Case dismissed."

Southern Cross Australia.

■ *"THERE'S NO DENYING I've got the greatest mind of the century," Thomas Harvey told an audience at the Wistar Institute, Pennsylvania, "but the trouble is, at my age, I'm afraid of losing it. That's why I keep it in the closet."*

Dr Harvey, 81, a pathologist from Lawrence, Kansas, was displaying exhibits from his private collection: "I performed the autopsy on Albert Einstein, and I've kept his brain in formaldehyde ever since. As you can see, I've still got it, but I have to admit Albert's rather gone to pieces of late.

"Now that I've retired, I'm trying to find a good home for it before I die. I had hoped to donate it to the Wistar Institute, to add to your collection of 200 famous brains, but I'd want an assurance that you'd look after it better than you did Walt Whitman's. A lab technician admitted to me earlier that he'd dropped Walt's on the floor a few years back, and had to flush him away with a hose. An ignominious end for America's greatest poet. I shouldn't like Albert to go the same way." *Wall Street Journal.*

■ *"IF WE CAN CATCH this Mitchell guy, we'll throw the book at him," Police Officer Morgan Fletcher assured Nashville reporters. "We're not sure if what he's doing actually is rape, because the women all consent, but we're bound to be able to get him on something. It could be rape by fraud."*

The wanted man, Raymond Mitchell III, 45, has become known in the Nashville area as Captain Fantasy. "He phones women late at night, pretending to be their boyfriend. He says he has a head cold, which is why he sounds strange. He then tells them to unlock their door, undress, put on a blindfold, smear their nipples with Jello, then wait for him in bed. Then he comes in, has sex with them, and leaves again. One woman let him do this twice a week for two months before she found out that it wasn't her boyfriend on the phone. Or on her." Associated Press.

"I HAVE INSPECTED Chan's underwear and confirm there is no wiring around his body," television personality Anthony Tang told the audience at a Daoist training centre in Hong Kong. "No trickery, no sleight of hand. What you are about to witness is *Qi gong*, a demonstration of pure penis power."

Tan then introduced the audience to Chan Tze-tan, 49, a Daoist philosopher, martial arts expert and fortune cookie manufacturer, who told them: "I have devoted my life to learning ancient Chinese techniques of regulating the body's energy, known as *Qi gong*, and have mastered the art of lifting weights with my penis. I began lifting small weights when I was 10, but it was only in 1982, when I attained insight into universal energy, Dao, that I learned to concentrate it in my vital manhood, and could attempt the feats you will witness today."

After warming-up by swinging 45kg discs back and forth with his genitalia, Chan removed his underwear for a final inspection. He then tied several red ropes to his penis and testicles, attached 159kg of weights to the end, breathed deeply several times, and lifted the metal discs 12cm off the ground for a period of 10 seconds. After a stunned silence, his audience respectfully left the hall.

Speaking after the demonstration, Chan confided: "I do not use chalk. My techniques are not only for weight-lifting. I can also cure impotence, premature ejaculation, and bed-wetting. I have 25 disciples at present, who also work at my cookie factory, and they can all lift 13kg with their private parts. We meet on Thursdays at 8.00pm in Temple Street. Admission is free."

Eastern Express.

● FOR SEVERAL MONTHS prior to the launch of its Science Fiction Channel, a cable TV company in Columbia, South Carolina, occupied the empty screen by pointing a camera at a fish tank. When the SF channel finally began broadcasting, thousands of angry viewers phoned in to complain, saying the fishies were better than the proper programmes and demanding the return of the tank. The aquarium has now been given its own show, which is pulling in high ratings and is transmitted for fourteen hours a day. *The Globe and Mail.*

■ **"IT WAS THE** hot bath that did it," pensioner Ron Tupper told a local reporter, as members of the Eastbourne Fire Brigade struggled to free him. "Hot water's always made my apricots sag, and that's where the problem started."

Tupper, a resident of Old Orchard Road, Eastbourne, explained what had happened to him that morning: "I'd just got out of the bath, and thought I'd sun myself on the patio before I got dressed. I sat down on a chair with the *Daily Express*, but my balls sack was loose because of the hot water, and my tessies slipped between the slats of the seat. I didn't pay any heed at first but, when I tried to stand, the skin had tightened up again, and I couldn't get them out.

"Realising I was stuck, I scuttled back into the house on the chair, and phoned the fire brigade. They were here for over an hour. They tried greasing me and all sorts, but it was no good. So they hacked the chair to pieces, which is a pity because it's one of a set I bought from Timothy Whites, and you can't get them anymore. It's cold showers for me from now on."

Eastbourne Herald.

"I DO NOT THINK it's disrespectful in the least," Kestutis Murauskas told a press conference in Vilnius. "In fact, the old Soviet leaders should be honoured to still be of service to the Lithuanian people."

Murauskas, business manager of the Grigikes Paper Factory, was exhibiting his firm's latest product to reporters: "Our new lavatory paper is made entirely from old Soviet bank notes, which went out of circulation after our country became independent. The material is very absorbent, which gives it excellent wiping properties, and, what with the rate of inflation we had back then, they're probably more valuable now than when they were legal tender. And the banks are delighted, because their vaults are finally being emptied of hundreds of tons of worthless currency.

"The notes had pictures of Gorbachev on them and, in spite of the recycling process, you can still make out his face quite clearly on most of them, even his birthmark. Somehow, the whole situation seems to sum up perfectly the feelings of Lithuanians towards the former Soviet Union."

Washington Times.

■ **"IN RETROSPECT, lighting the match was my big mistake. But I was only trying to retrieve the gerbil," Vito Bustone told bemused doctors in the Severe Burns Unit of Salt Lake City Hospital.**

Bustone, and his homosexual partner Kiki Rodriguez, had been admitted for emergency treatment after a felching session had gone seriously wrong. "I pushed a cardboard tube up his rectum and slipped Faggot, our gerbil, in," he explained. "As usual, Kiki shouted out 'Armageddon', my cue that he'd had enough. I tried to retrieve Faggot but he wouldn't come out again, so I peered into the tube and struck a match, thinking the light might attract him."

At a hushed press conference, a hospital spokesman described what happened next. "The match ignited a pocket of intestinal gas and a flame shot up the tube, igniting Mr Bustone's moustache and severely burning his face. It also set fire to the gerbil's fur and whiskers which, in turn, ignited a larger pocket of gas further up the intestine, propelling the rodent out like a cannonball."

Bustone suffered second degree burns and a broken nose from the impact of the gerbil, while Rodriguez suffered first and second degree burns to his anus and lower intestinal tract. Sheriff Hugo Root later told reporters: "It's Faggot I feel sorry for. Being stuffed up some queen's tradesman's entrance..."

Bloomberg News Service.

"HOW DARE YOU accuse us of theft? Clearly, shoddy workmanship is the culprit here," the police chief of Manila told an astonished news conference.

General Generoso Necesito had called the conference to explain how more than half a ton of marijuana, cocaine and amphetamines had disappeared from police evidence lockers during the last year. "Rats and cockroaches got in through gaps in the locker doors and ate it all, every last scrap," he claimed. "We know this to be a fact, because the cockroaches at police headquarters have been behaving very oddly. They just stand there looking dazed when we shine a light on them, instead of scuttling off into a dark corner. Obviously they have been getting high on drugs."

When a reporter produced photographs of police officers selling drugs on the black market, the General became furious. "You are the filth of the earth. I have told the truth. No one will believe your absurd allegations and, if you print them, arrests will follow." The press conference was hastily adjourned.

Toronto Star.

"JULY 25, 1993. 7.00AM: Cleaned out the tub and scraped my feet with my fingernails to remove layers of dead skin. 7.05: Passed a large, firm stool, and a pint of urine. Used 5 sheets of paper. 7.10: Shaved for the third time with a Gillette Atra II blade and threw it away."

Robert Shields, a former minister and English teacher, was reading extracts from his (currently) forty-million-word diary to a small audience in Dayton, Washington State. During the introduction to his readings, he explained his working practices. "It was 1972 when I decided to record the rest of my life in five-minute increments. Since then I've kept details of every expense, every trip, every conversation, every mail delivery, every bowel movement, every sexual occurrence, everything. I'm completely uninhibited. I've found dozens of ways to describe urination and the smell of different sorts of body gas. Taped to the pages are fingernails, bits of dead skin, nose hairs complete with residue, grocery receipts, meat labels, anything that comes to hand. I spend about eight hours a day making notes, and another two hours typing them up on three IBM memory typewriters. I don't have much time for anything else, so a lot of the diary is filled with stuff about me writing the diary."

Throughout the performance, Shields stopped speaking every five minutes in order to make further notes. Asked why he did it, he replied: "This is my bid for immortality. I thought of becoming a serial killer. Surely this is a better course?"

Eastern Express.

● "DINING AT THE Nha Hang Bia Hoi restaurant in Hanoi earlier this year was an unforgettable experience," Jonathan Cartwright told readers of the *Far Eastern Economic Review*. "And, believe me, I should know. I've certainly tried to forget it plenty of times since.

"When the waiter brought me the menu, it included unripe corncob soup, fried flour-coated frog, and fricasseed bull genitalia. Among the *amuse bouche* were very unamusing salted crickets, small packets of dung beetles, and giant red ants' eggs in a salad. Dog came in two styles, kebabed and steamed, and veal came in four styles — only kindled, burned, badly burned with raw lemon leaf, and burned with burned rice flour. But the piece de resistance was undoubtedly the *not born yet dead cow baby — stir fried*. A Western journalist at another table passed out when she read that."

The Far Eastern Economic Review.

"BRUCE JENSEN is just incredibly naive," prosecutor Bill McGuire informed reporters in Bountiful, Utah. "You've got a situation here where love is unbelievably blind."

McGuire was speaking following the arrest of Jensen's "wife", Felix Urioste, on fraud charges. "The couple got married in 1991, after a single sexual encounter, because Urioste claimed he was pregnant and Jensen felt responsible. After the wedding, he said he'd had a miscarriage, and the marriage was basically celibate after that. Urioste got away with it because Jensen never saw him naked, he was taking female hormones that gave him slight breasts and, on the few occasions when they did have sex, he secretly fashioned a rubber vagina out of a washing machine hose, and placed it between his legs. Even so, he has a thick moustache and beard, and a normal size penis, but Jensen loved his wife and gave her the benefit of the doubt. Things were okay until April, when Urioste disappeared, along with a walletful of credit cards, and Jensen was heartbroken. He's just a little country bumpkin from Wyoming that wouldn't hurt a flea. When we finally arrested Urioste in Las Vegas, he'd run up $40,000 in bills. It's a sad story."

Jensen later admitted: "I feel pretty stupid. It trashes you out to believe everything a person says and find out they lied to you on basically 100% of it. The moustache should have given him away, but my mother had one and that was virtually a handlebar. Some women do, you know. I find them quite attractive."

Eastern Express.

"THESE STORIES FLY in the face of common sense," Phra Dharmamatanobhas told a press conference in Bangkok. "How could anyone have sex on the deck of a ferry in Scandinavia in winter? It would be too cold to get an erection."

Phra Dharmamatanobhas was defending a fellow Buddhist monk, Phra Yantra Amaro Bikhu, against accusations of repeatedly breaking his vow of celibacy. "There has been a misunderstanding. Phra Yantra is innocent. He only lets men near him, and always keeps women at a distance. True, there are pictures of him getting into the back of a van with a woman harpist, but he merely did this to demonstrate advanced

Tantric positions to her. Furthermore, the DNA test demanded by the Belgrade woman in the paternity suit was obviously faulty, and the Stavanger ferry incident only took place in the fevered, opium-inspired imagination of a Cambodian nun, Kaewta Mongchinda, who deserves to be punished in the deepest hell.

"But people should understand the temptations we monks must endure in the modern world. As soon as we look heavenwards in prayer, we see advertisements for women's undergarments. Many of us use rotting corpse contemplation to surmount lust, and I agree with the prosecution that the monk who was caught having sex with a corpse during funeral rites did wrong. But do not tar us all with the same brush." *The Sydney Morning Herald.*

EMPLOYMENT — YOUR WEEK AHEAD.

FRIDAY: If your interviewer is male, it may be easier for you to achieve success. Why not bring along your girl-friend? The ox should avoid the goat and horse.

SATURDAY: Excellent! The positive forces of a lucky day are here. Be sure to wear yellow trousers and black jewellery. Yellow underwear too! No squid for lunch though. If you attend an interview given by a dog, you shall receive good news. Tigers should avoid the monkey and snake.

MONDAY: If you don't mind, dress up in a yellow suit, shirt, and tie and even stockings, gentlemen! Dragons should avoid the dog and the rabbit.

TUESDAY: Attend your interview with a monkey and success will simply fall into your hands. Snakes should avoid the pig and the tiger.

WEDNESDAY: Want to succeed? Then bring all the female members of your family to your interview. Success will be guaranteed! Horses should avoid the rat and the ox.

Eastern Super Job [Hong Kong].

"I AM QUITE FINE and not feeling any discomfort, thank you," Michael Balama told concerned villagers, "but regretfully, I feel unable to come down just at the moment."

Balama, a 45-year-old farmer from Pankshin, Nigeria, had been located atop an olive tree two kilometres from his home. According to Odundu Odwilly, his former employer: "This tree nonsense has gone on too long. Five years ago Balama climbed up a locust-bean tree in front of his house, and refused to come down. Villagers, priests and traditional healers all pleaded with him, year after year, but without any success. Two weeks ago, we finally persuaded him to descend, but now he's gone up an even taller one."

Balama was eventually found after the entire village launched a manhunt for him. "I do not know what I am doing up this tree," he told village elders. "I would dearly love to come down, but some people are holding me, and preventing me from doing so." After being told that he was clearly the only person in the tree, Balama enforced a vomit over the head of Mr Odwilly and hurled olives at elders and the women, forcing them to make a tactical retreat.

The Star Tonight.

"TODAY'S WEDDING was a lavish affair, and the bride looked radiant in a pink silk dress," Chu Kuo reported on Heilongjiang TV's *Evening News*. "In fact, the whole ceremony went very well, considering that she had been dead for a week."

Speaking from the morgue in Harbin city hospital, Heilongjiang province, Chu described the circumstances leading up to the unorthodox wedding which had just taken place there: "Twenty-five-year old Ge had been courting Yu for several years, but he was reluctant to commit himself to marriage. Yu became pregnant, and her family insisted that Ge had to marry her. But a Canadian uncle arranged a job for Ge as a short-order chef for McDonald's in Montreal, so he told Yu that he was ending their relationship. 'If you go abroad and do not marry me, I will kill myself,' his girlfriend warned and, after Ge showed her the airplane ticket to Canada he'd already bought, she swallowed a hundred sleeping pills. 'They are candy,' said Ge as he waved her good-bye. Three hours later she was dead.

"Despite the unfortunate circumstances, her furious family still insisted on a proper marriage, with photographs, music, a conjurer, and hired cars to bring family members to the service. So Ge finally relented, bought a ring, booked the morgue, and married Yu, who remained in her coffin throughout. Ge took her ashes to the Honeymoon Hotel at the Niagara Falls. Her family are now content."

The Herald [Zimbabwe].

■ **A MAN WHO THOUGHT** the NHS sex change waiting list was too long decided to perform the operation himself in a quiet West Country lane. In the privacy of his pink three-wheeler car, he severed his penis with a Stanley knife and threw it into a hedge.

Dressed in tights, high heels and a mini skirt, and bleeding profusely after his DIY amputation, he was found by Shirley Spurr of Chilworthy, who called an ambulance. "I'm not easily shocked because I lived in Uganda under Amin, but frankly it was a bit surprising. You don't expect this sort of thing in such a quiet part of North Devon," she said.

The penis was retrieved by a farmer, packed in ice, and rushed to North Devon District Hospital, together with its owner. A spokesman said the man's condition was "comfortable". There are no plans to reunite the separated couple. *Western Morning News.*

"OF COURSE I DON'T know whether any disabled people would actually want to perform naked in the shower," Ron Shitega told reporters. "But if people perform in it, then it's a stage. And if it's a stage, it's got to have wheelchair access."

Shitega, chief of the Disabled Access Division of the Los Angeles Department of Building, was welcoming a ruling by the Appeals Commission against the Odd Ball Cabaret and Strip Club on Sepulveda Boulevard: "There's one part of the club where customers can pay $20 to sit in front of a glass panel and watch a naked woman taking a shower while she dances to music. What we say is that, if an able-bodied person can get up there and perform, then disabled people should be able to get up there and perform as well. So either the club builds a ramp for them, or else we close it down."

Asked whether anyone was likely to pay $20 to watch a paraplegic dance naked, Shitega snapped: "Why not? Are you saying that disabled people aren't beautiful? Wheelchair dancing is beautiful. Anyway, the alloy they use for the wheels nowadays doesn't rust like it used to. It's a great idea. And, yeah, criminals on Death Row could choose to bow out this way, by going into the shower on electrically operated wheelchairs. That way at least they'd die with a smile and a stiffy. Get real."
The Washington Times.

Prisoner: Shut up, fucking poofter. You poofter, thank you.
His Honour: You just keep quiet, we will have a word with you in a moment.
Prisoner: Fuck to you. All right, you poofter. All right, I fuck you. That is answer.
His Honour: It is said that you assaulted...
Prisoner: Fuck the English, fuck the colony, all right.
His Honour: If you don't shut up...
Prisoner: Fuck the judge too. That is not true.
His Honour: Do we assume this is a plea of not guilty?
Defence Lawyer: Yes, I think we can assume that.
Prisoner: I fuck you, answer you, stuff you, poofter. Is that enough for you answer?
His Honour: That is no answer, but I assume that the outrageous torrent of language from the accused is a plea of not guilty. Remanded for trial. Has someone been imprudent enough to grant a bail agreement?
Defence Lawyer: I hesitate to ask him.
Prisoner: Fuck you.
His Honour: Do you wish to ask for bail?
Prisoner: You ask yourself bail, poofter. Now ask me.
His Honour: I don't have to ask.
Prisoner: Fuck the bail, fuck Australia.
His Honour: I take it, then, you don't wish to seek bail.
Prisoner: Stuff that.
His Honour: No application for bail. The accused is remanded for trial in custody.
Prisoner: Fucking bastard, poofter melon-arse.

Transcript of interchange between Judge Roy Grubb and defendant Yusif Biyikli at Adelaide Criminal Court.

"THIS TOAD MADNESS must cease at once," Environment Minister Dr Mok Mareth declared to astonished Cambodian viewers during a party political broadcast. "Toads create balance in the ecosystem, and should be left to catch harmful insects that destroy crops in the field. Tens of thousands have been killed in recent months so, from this day forth, drinking the crushed fermented toad will become a punishable offence."

Traditional healers in Phnom Penh, like Chay Seang Y, reacted angrily to the broadcast: "Toad wine is especially good for syphilis, and many other kinds of sexually transmitted diseases, eases the pain of piles and promotes good appetite and sleep. We only use fresh farmed toads which we buy at the market. We peel off the skin, dry them, fry them, crush them, and brew them with rice, wine and herbs. Toad wine can cure impotence, and it is even better than gecko wine at chasing viruses out of the blood. It is also a much cheaper way to enjoy alcohol than beer or whisky. That's why it is so popular."

A government spokesman confirmed that two psycho-active drugs, dimethyltryptamine and bufotenine, are found in significant quantities in toads. *Phnom Penh Post.*

"BY YOUR ACTIONS, you have brought ridicule and contempt on yourself," Judge Giles Rooke told Anthony Akhurst in a hushed Crown Court at Canterbury. "It is very rare indeed to find this offence being committed with the defendant putting himself on the receiving end."

Earlier, prosecuting counsel Mr Oliver Saxby had described the events that led to the arrest of Akhurst, 45, on a charge of attempted buggery with his family pet's alsatian. "On the evening of the offence, when the defendant returned home from the pub, his two sons were in bed, and his wife was at work. At about 11.30pm, the elder son heard the family dog, Bruno, yelping excitedly, so he went downstairs. There he saw his father, naked on his hands and knees, and the dog standing behind him on its hind legs, thrusting vigorously, its front paws on top of his father's back. Realising he had been observed, the defendant claimed it was all part of Bruno's training, and advised his son to say nothing to his mother. But next day his son told a teacher and, when police began making enquiries, Akhurst eventually confessed the truth."

Akhurst, who admitted similar previous offenses, was bound over for 18 months. His barrister, Mr David Burles, told the court in mitigation that, since his arrest, Akhurst had lost his job, been beaten up in his local pub and, worst of all, now lives alone in Margate.

Thanet Times.

"WHAT IS THIS JOKE?" shouted I.H. Gilada, brandishing an unfurled condom in the faces of delegates of the World Health Organisation in Bombay. "As a medical man of thirty years experience, I tell you this is a sheath for a donkey, not for a man."

Dr Gilada was protesting about a consignment of five million South Korean condoms, distributed free throughout western India by the WHO, in an attempt to combat AIDS. "They are six centimetres longer and three centimetres wider than our most popular local brand, Norodh, and they are useless. Every day, my surgery is full of women who have got one lodged inside, because it fell off during intercourse. Prostitutes refuse to use them, even though they are free. Why are they so big? It is well-known that Korean gentlemen are more petite than average all points south of the navel. This is their revenge on the manhood of India."

The Gazette [Zimbabwe].

"DO NOT BE TEMPTED by the lure of easy kwachas," Ellen Muluzi warned women in a lecture in the Town Hall, Lilongwe. "Such repugnant and stinking behaviour only drags the fine name of Malawi down to the sordid level of Zambia."

Muluzi was speaking about the Zambian craze for dog sex videos, which has recently spread to Malawi: "Azungus [white men] no longer want sex with African women. Instead they prefer to pay the women K500 and ask them to have sex with their dogs, while the Azungus film the event on camcorders. Zambian women are always being asked by foreigners to perform bizarre acts with dogs in hotel bedrooms and they agree, because they'd do anything for money and Zambian men don't have any. But our women must never sink so low as to have sex with a dog, even if means getting thousands and thousands of kwachas."

Replying on behalf of Zambian women, Janet Karim, editor-in-chief of *The Independent*, dismissed the entire story as "fucking unrealistic. If you ask me, Ellen Muluzi is a bit of a dog herself. But it's unlikely anyone would pay to have sex with her, or want to video it."

The Chronicle [Malawi].

■ "I AM SHOCKED to have to tell you that government officials and school inspectors are very fond of having casual sex with the schoolchildren they are supposed to be supervising," President Phineas Magagula of the Swaziland National Association of Teachers told the Minister of Education Senator Arthur Khoza during a conference at Salesian High School, Manzini. "It seems that their job is to propose love to the students when they visit the schools, instead of carrying out their required duties. I therefore demand that all officials are issued with free condoms and given this message: 'When seducing children: No love bites. Two inputs only (tradesman's entrance is out of bounds). Please wear a condom.' This will prevent the spread of venereal disease and quell indiscipline in schools. Thank you for your time, Minister, and God bless you."

President Magagula has since been relieved of his duties.

The Times of Swaziland.

"IT IS SIMPLY a question of supply and demand," a doctor at the Sin Hua clinic in Shenzen told reporters. "We carry out hundreds of abortions each month, and many Chinese women like to eat foetuses as a tonic. What is your problem with this?"

The doctor was speaking to reporters from Hong Kong, who were investigating the latest health food fad in China. "Eating a three-month-old foetus can make your skin smoother, your body stronger, and it is especially good for the kidneys. We are a state-run clinic, so we give the foetuses away to anyone who asks for them. Charging for them would be unethical. Yes, I regularly eat foetus. I'm also partial to fried afterbirth. Personally, I would recommend both dishes with pork soup."

The Korea Herald.

SUNDAY BEAMS **by Dr. Philip M. Kajura**.

Gemini (May 21-June 20): Avoid cribbing an answer from your fellow classmate. Do not be a person who is habitually dishonest.

Cancer (June 21-July 20): You may hear some news about a man whose wife has committed adultery. Also you are advised not to make a cuckold by having sex with another man.

Scorpio (October 23-November 22): You may be feeling unwell as a result of eating or drinking too much on Sunday, Wednesday and Saturday. Do you know that you are a lovely creature?

Capricorn (December 21-January 19): This is not a week of forgery. Do not forget to feed your animals on time. Beware all mindreaders. They cause sickness and bends.

Pisces (February 19-March 20): You are advised to avoid brutal punishments. Things are not as bad as you think, except on Monday and Wednesday.

Aries (March 21-April 20): Your house needs a fresh paint. Avoid caressing the sexual organs or kissing before sexual intercourse. Do not stand outside in the cold if your health is not well.

Dr Kajura says, "Why not consult me for advice? Come with confidence and I will help you out of jam. Write PO Box 8692, Dar es Salaam, and buy your Kiswahili book *Siri ya Maisha Yako Price 1,000/-"*.

Sunday News [Tanzania].

"FHUKUR BALAK is not dead, he is in Samadhi," Chitta Sikdar repeatedly told a bemused delegation of doctors from the Calcutta Health Authority. "Your medical schools teach you nothing of the light which trembles within us all."

The delegation was demanding access to the body of Guru Fhukur Balak, which had been lying on blocks of ice in an air-conditioned room in his ashram since May 5th. Although several doctors had pronounced him dead six weeks earlier, his 1,500 followers insisted he was still alive, and refused to allow a cremation.

"When I pointed out that complete absence of heartbeat and breathing was a certain indication of the total cessation of life," said one official, "they became abusive. Then they apologised and told me it was due to his deep meditative state, and that he had promised to rise again next Tuesday. When Tuesday came and nothing happened, they told us gurus did not keep diaries and refused to let us take the body. I said, you've got an answer for everything but, mark my words, that man is dead."

"If he has not returned to his body by Diwali, you may have a case," Mr Sikdar conceded, "but we all know your real motives. You are on a commission from the crematorium." *Khaleej Times.*

● **"THE TOILET REFLECTS the history and temperament of a people," moderator Pao Ping-Wing reminded delegates at the International Symposium on Public Lavatories in Hong Kong. "The Chinese are traditionally very conservative, so their toilets are private. In Japan the toilets are very open, and the Japanese language has more than 650 expressions to describe the task of visiting the toilet. In Bangkok, commuters even carry portable toilets in their car, with a car battery connector enabling them to flush. But, if the culture of the toilet differs, the universal need does not."**

Later, Urban Council chairman Dr Ronald Leung Ding-Bong addressed the most serious problem facing delegates: "There is a need for more female toilets or we are sure to have a disaster. Take a look anywhere and you will see that the queue for the ladies is too long. It would be much easier if only men used toilets, but we are now studying what takes women so long. We have found that 60% of women hover above the toilet, and 20% nest by placing paper on the seat. The rest, in my opinion, are out to kill themselves. Public toilets are a dangerous place for those who sit or squat. This is no joke, and I'm giving you a warning, ladies, you could end up in the casualty department. People still climb up on the pedestal toilets, so I am a big advocate of the squatters. Not so far to fall."

South China Morning Post.

"I'VE MADE SOME weird arrests in my time but this even beats the woman shoplifting with a rabid donkey for protection last month," Sergeant Paulo Quadros of the Belo Ilorizonte police force told reporters. "This time, it took twelve of us, including eight firemen, and we had to take a dozen floorboards into custody as well."

Sergeant Quadros was answering questions about the arrest of Sergio De Sa, on charges of aggravated theft. "De Sa is a glue sniffer, who steals from shops to feed his habit. On Saturday night he broke into the Gola Gola glue factory, but he lost control when he saw the really good stuff, and started inhaling directly from the vats. Of course, he was overcome by fumes after one sniff and lost his balance, upsetting a vat of glue as he fell. By the time he came round, he was stuck to the floor, and had to lie there helplessly till the workers turned up on Monday morning. They couldn't shift him and, in the end, we had to get power saws and cut round him. The factory's lost a day's production and he's lost the skin off his back.

"While we were formally charging him, he said it was worth losing his skin because Gola Gola Quickstix was the *premier cru* of glue. What is it with these people? Are they nuts? Last month, we arrested another guy with tubes stuck right up both nostrils. He died in custody. Somebody called him Walrus Face, and he laughed so much he haemorrhaged."
O Globo.

● "SO WHAT IF A FEW people are embarrassed?" Ze'ev Lichtenzon told reporters. "They'd be a damn sight more embarrassed if they got an exhaust pipe rammed up their recti."

Lichtenzon was speaking after his advertising campaign provoked a storm of outrage across Tel Aviv. "I got pig sick of all the bad driving and traffic accidents in this city. It's been proved scientifically by me that most accidents are caused by men with penises less than five inches long and no self-control. That's why I rented 300 billboards to get my anti-machismo message across. ROWDY DRIVERS HAVE SMALL PENISES is one slogan, FAST DRIVERS ARE PREMATURE EJACULATORS is another, BIG CAR, SMALL MAN is a third. The most successful one so far is RESEARCH PROVES IT: TOO FAST ON THE ROAD, TOO FAST IN BED, with an automatic foam spurter fitted to it. I've been getting burning rags through my letterbox, so it's obviously doing the trick.

"Next, I'm going to target women. They're even worse drivers than the men. That's because they don't have any penises at all. It's all there in Freud." *The Jerusalem Post.*

"WE'VE OFFERED to change the 'Mc' to 'Mac' but you can't argue with these people," solicitor Jim Unkles told reporters outside the federal court in Melbourne. "They just keep telling us to get our tits out, and they won't listen to reason."

Unkles was acting on behalf of "McTits", a takeaway shop that had opened in January amid protests by women's groups. "It's a ridiculous action for the McDonalds Corporation to bring," he said, "There's no possible confusion. My client is part Scottish, and his female staff wear nothing except see-through aprons when they serve customers. Hence the name, McTits. Simple. McDonalds says McTits is trading off their success, but that's ridiculous. The word 'Tits' looks nothing like 'Donalds', and you could hardly confuse the two places. I mean, the only buns you'll see in McDonalds are the ones with sesame seeds on top.

"My client and his staff stand firm on their right to trade under their own name, but, honestly, our girls would do anything to resolve the problem. They'd bend over backwards to help. If you get my drift."

Bangkok Post.

■ **"WHAT HAPPENED will haunt me for ever," Julius Mwinyi of the Seventh Day Adventist church told the Coroner's Court in Dar es Salaam. "One minute they were chanting 'Our faith in the Lord will sustain us,' next they had suddenly disappeared below the surface."**

Mwinyi, 43, described the events leading up to the tragedy which was believed to have claimed eighteen lives. "We were all on a pilgrimage, setting out in a flotilla of canoes across Lake Victoria to a religious festival at Mwanza. We started singing hymns. However, some ruffians in a passing cruiser shouted obscenities at us, and suggested that we should all test our faith by walking on the water like Jesus. Our minister shouted back, telling them that he would do just that. Next thing, seventeen unfortunate souls stood up in their canoes, cried out 'Allelujah', then joined hands with the minister and began chanting. Then they stepped out of their canoes and sunk like stones. The police spent three days recovering bodies, but never found them all. It's the crocodiles you see. I suppose crocodiles are God's creatures, but all the same I'd wipe them out. Anyway, my faith remains unshaken."

San Francisco Chronicle.

"WHY DON'T YOU strap me securely to the operating table? I have a name for you, Doctor Neuberger," declared Roger Lavancier, while giving evidence to the High Court in Versailles. "It is Sparky the ten-thumbed moron."

Dr Philippe Neuberger was accused by Lavancier, 75, of having failed in his professional duty during an operation at a hospital in the Yvelines to remove an anal polyp. Prosecuting counsel M. Gerber told the court: "Dr Neuberger insisted on using a new technique of removal by electro-coagulation, claiming that it avoided bleeding. But, during the course of the operation, a spark from the electric scalpel ignited the residual methane gas in M. Lavancier's intestines. The force of the resulting explosion blew him clean off the operating table, causing him to collide with a trolley on which M. Bluare was being wheeled in for a routine vasectomy reversal. Both men sustained near-fatal injuries.

"My client has been 28% handicapped ever since, and is demanding FF950,000 in compensation. Worst of all, after the operation was over, his own doctor discovered that the polyp was still there. If that were not ironic enough, M. Bluare has since had to have his testicles removed." Nice Matin.

"YES, IT'S TRUE that some people have called me a bimbo, slut and whore," Annabel Chong told Los Angeles reporters as she embarked on her latest world record attempt. "Jerry Falwell even said that I should 'be buried in a Y-shaped coffin', but they're all completely wrong. It's just that I enjoy my body, and so do my men."

Ms Chong, 22, a Singapore-born sociology student and pornographic actress, was attempting to set a new sex record by having intercourse with 300 men in ten hours. "My advertisement for volunteers drew 12,700 replies from all over the world, especially Sweden and Germany. The chosen 300 have all been told to bring an AIDS certificate and a condom with them when they report to reception. I've planned the event like a Roman orgy, with me dressed as an Egyptian princess and the men in togas. Each man has only been allotted 90 seconds to perform, so I've arranged for five women to stand by, to act as warm-ups and to avoid bottlenecks.

"I'll be taking a break every two hours to fix my make-up. I've never made love to more than twelve men simultaneously before, but I'm not afraid of hard work so I'm confident of success. Even if a few volunteers fail to rise to the occasion, I shall still smash the existing record. I asked a Mr McWhirter at the Guinness Book of Records to officiate, and to join in if he so wished, but he has not returned my call."

Sunday Morning Post [Hong Kong].

"BEWARE. A gang of charlatans has been at work in our city boasting that they possess the ancient secret of penis enlargement," said Dr Thongchai Termprasith to the press, after more than a hundred Thai men had reported to Chiang Mai's Maharaj Hospital with severe genital disorders, within the space of a few days.

"Those men are nothing more than quacks and the results of their handiwork are woeful to behold. They charge 500 Baht, and use a knitting needle to inject the member with their 'magic potion', which turns out to be a mixture of olive oil, chalk, kapok and other rubbish. I've even seen bits of the Bangkok telephone directory. Naturally, the penis swells up to the size of a loofah, which is when money is handed over. But after a few days a most terrible thing happens. The men start to experience a dreadful burning after intercourse, and soon their manhood turns rotten and implodes. I myself have amputated more than twenty this week."

One victim, who wished to remain anonymous, told the press: "Learn from my misfortunes. I am bereft. Last week I thought twelve centimetres was not enough to satisfy my wife. How will I pleasure her with no centimetres?"

"Be happy with the Natural One that God has given you," Dr Thongchai told reporters, "and remember that a healthy maggot is better by far than a gangrenous king cobra."

Bangkok Post.

"WE WEREN'T BEING inhumane to the dogs, only to disk jockeys," a spokesman for the Los Angeles radio station KROQ-FM said in a press statement. "Tilles is the most stupid, egotistical DJ I've ever worked with. He must have been insane to sign a contract with the network agreeing to give up his rights as a human being."

A planned publicity stunt by the station had been halted by the city's Department of Animal Regulation after complaints from pet lovers. Fellow radio presenters Kevin Ryder and Bean Baxter explained: "We dressed Jay 'Kebab' Tilles in a bite suit, and wrapped him completely in hunks of beef. We got three pit bull terriers ready and were about to let them loose and see what happened when these goddamn officials appeared and told us we'd be violating state law if we carried on.

"It's crazy. They told us we'd be accused of worrying the dogs. But the dogs weren't worried, they were loving every minute of it. Tilles *was* a little worried though. But he'd already told us he'd do anything to break into television. He's a very sad man really." *UPI.*

■ **"THE AYATOLLAH has spoken. The fatwa against Barbie dolls has been decreed and will therefore commence immediately," a director from the College of Islamic Sharia told reporters at a Kuwait press conference. "Barbie resembles a mature woman and has nothing to do with childhood.**

This she-devil has polished nails, and wears shameful clothing and skirts high above the knee. Our children must be protected from this evil Western style of living, in the shaping of the body, the voluptuous fullness of the lips, and the blonde styling of the hair."

The pronouncement of the fatwa has met with mixed reactions in the Middle East. Scholars from the Cairo-based Al-Azhar condemned it as "generally incorrect. We hereby grant Barbie a clean bill of health". But several toy shops have been fire-bombed by protestors, following which the local distributor issued this statement: "In the event that the fatwa is to be carried out, I require clarification on a theological matter. Does the fatwa also include Barbie's friend Ken? And may I still sell Sindy?"
Middle East Marketing Intelligence Report.

"IS THERE NO JUSTICE left in Taita Taveta?" demanded Peter Wambugu Mugo in Nyahururu central court. "You accuse me of wickedness, but if I'd killed the sheep and sold it to the butcher, you'd all have queued up to buy a bit."

Inspector Odhiambo, prosecuting, told the court how Mugo, who was accused of abducting a sheep and having carnal knowledge of it, had been caught in flagrante delicto. "The complainant left his four sheep grazing but, on returning later, found only three. Searching in a nearby copse, he saw the missing sheep tethered to a bush, dressed in a nappy and a baby bonnet, with the madman Mugo standing behind it, naked, singing a lullaby and thrusting in time to the music. The alarm was raised and he was overpowered by furious members of the public."

Defending himself, Mugo told the Senior Resident Magistrate, Mrs Manjiru Karanja, that he had decided to go with animals because he could no longer afford VD treatment. "Five times I go with women, five times I get VD" he declared. "It is time people realised that animals are safer and cheaper."

Mugo also pleaded not guilty to a charge of urinating into an ashtray in Barclay's Bank, Voi Town, claiming that he had a weak bladder and was being held prisoner by the bank manager at the time. He was found guilty on all counts, fined Sh800, and sentenced to two years imprisonment plus two strokes of the cane.

Kenya Times.

■ *"AND THEREFORE, YOUR HONOUR, the allegation of indecent exposure levelled against my client is clearly without foundation, and I ask for the charge to be dismissed."*

Solicitor Lisa Cooper was speaking on behalf of Ian Roberts, 53, a science lecturer from Cambridge, Mass., who had earlier given his version of events to the court: "This is all a simple misunderstanding. My wife's washing machine was defective in the rinse cycle, and the soap powder in my underpants caused a rash on my genitals. This made them itch, so I started letting them hang out of my briefs. Unfortunately, during a tutorial with Michelle Sowden-Frost, I caught a whiff of her perfume, which caused my penis to become erect and, even more unfortunately, I had unwittingly left open my fly. My erection protruded through my lab coat, and here I am. Incidentally, we have now purchased a new washing machine."

The magistrate accepted Mr Roberts' explanation of events, and cleared him of all charges. *North Shore News [Vancouver].*

"THE INCIDENT has confirmed my worst fears about Jacques Delors and the Single Market," said Beryl Tuber, speaking from her Medway bungalow. "Teddy Taylor is quite right, and from now on Kitty and I will be holidaying in the Lake District."

Kitty and Beryl Tuber, two widows in their late seventies, were returning from a pilgrimage to Lourdes when their car was stopped by French customs officials, after a tip-off that drugs, pornographic videos, and several boxes of latex dildoes had been hidden in their boot by smugglers. "I saw the boxes in the car boot," Beryl continued, "and I thought at first that Kitty must have bought something nice for our niece's pony, Pumplechook. But then the customs man started waving what looked like a large rolling pin in my face, and shouting 'Husband no good, eh?' and I replied 'My husband's dead', and started crying. Then he blew up what I thought was a beach ball, and it turned out to be a naked woman with blonde hair. That's when Kitty fainted."

A customs official later confirmed that gangs of smugglers often hide drugs and pornography in the cars of innocent tourists, in the hope of evading detection. The two women were eventually released without charge. *Overseas Job Express.*

“IT’S TRUE THAT, at present, the cleaning staff consists entirely of my wife and myself,” Ronald Leazenby admitted to reporters in Kokomo, Indiana. “However, we pay good rates, so we expect to attract some younger employees before long, and we’re convinced that NHS will soon be doing great business.”

Angela and Ronald Leazenby, former abattoir workers both now in their late sixties, were describing what clients could expect if they hired domestic cleaners from *Nude Housecleaning Services*. “For $50 an hour, a pair of male and/or female NHS employees will come to your house and do your laundry, wash floors, and do light dusting, fully nude. For $75, our staff will prance a little as they vacuum, and also climb onto furniture to dust pelmets. Our deluxe service costs $100 an hour, but that includes many extras, such as steam cleaning their upholstery, bending on request and the application of laundry pegs to wherever the client suggests. Such a service has not previously been available in the state of Indiana, and we believe it represents terrific value for money. Why the police keep raiding our premises is a mystery to me. As for the pig – I cure my own ham. And there’s an end to it.”

The Toronto Globe and Mail.

"THE WEATHER HAS been cancelled until further notice," newscaster Priya Suresh announced at the end of New Delhi's main evening news bulletin. "It's all got too complicated to explain, and we keep getting it wrong anyway. So instead, a little earlier than planned, here's *Cibaca Geet Mala*."

Justifying the sudden change in scheduling, a spokesman for Doordarshan Television later explained: "It's been an abnormal April with, quite literally, scorching sunshine one minute and bitter winds and rain the next. On Monday evening, our weatherman told viewers, quite literally, to keep their woollen underwear on, and next day the temperature was 102°. On Tuesday he promised more sunshine and we had four inches of snow. He's a professional meteorologist and, when the death threats from viewers came in, he took it all very personally. He spent all Wednesday quite literally memorising a long report, and tried to explain the freak conditions using satellite pictures but, half way through the evening broadcast, he forgot what he was talking about and, quite literally, he couldn't go on. He just kept smiling nervously and adjusting his tie while repeating 'If the snowcover over the Himalayas is sparse, it will surely lead to a good monsoon' until he started to cry and eventually we quite literally faded him out.

"We haven't seen him since. We'll try him again next month, though. It's always blazing hot every day in May, so he should be able to cope. But I'm not sure he will return. His granny was attacked by an irate farmer with a chainsaw. Quite literally."

The Sunday Times of India.

● **"WE HAVE NO clues yet about who the thief might be," Officer Ben Wilmott told reporters at an Auckland press conference, "but, frankly, I think he's probably been punished enough already. What happened to him shouldn't happen to a dog."**

Officer Wilmott had been called to an East Coast camp site by an elderly couple, Ted and Alice Fairbairn. "They'd heard sounds outside their mobile home in the night and thought someone was trying to steal petrol from the tank, but they were too frightened to investigate. Sure enough, in the morning they found a siphon hose and a petrol can on the ground outside their mobile, together with a pool of vomit and a metal cap. Only it wasn't the cap from the fuel tank, it was the one from the sewage holding tank. The guy had removed the cap from the wrong tank, stuck the rubber tube in, and started to siphon out the contents with his mouth.

"Sorry, but that's what I call a real sucker for punishment."

Southland Times [New Zealand].

"MY CLIENT HAS been seeking medical help for his condition," solicitor Anthony Muller told Wolverhampton Crown Court, "and apologises for any offence his behaviour has caused. But the fact is that, for several years now, he has been in the grip of a compulsion, and can only find sexual fulfilment by simulating sex in public with bin liners."

Muller was defending Karl Watkins, 23, an electrician who had pleaded guilty to seven charges of outraging public decency. "My client's fetish centres on the feel and touch of a bin liner. It started when, as a child, he used to get into a crouching position, push the pedal of a flip bin and rapidly spank himself with the lid. For some time, he has been prowling the streets at night, and the police have often surprised him in wheelie bins, and even in the backs of dustcarts. In fact, his absolute sexual fantasy is to be inside a dustcart, naked, when the bin bags are crushed. He very much regrets the incidents on pavements in Halesowen, Stourbridge, Blackheath and Brierley Hill, all of which involved him standing in front of teenage schoolgirls with his trousers and pants around his ankles, and simulating sex with bin bags."

Judge Malcolm Ward placed Watkins on probation for three years, on condition he took bromide or an equivalent drug to reduce his high sex drive. His girlfriend said she would stand by him, on condition that he no longer helped her to put out the garbage.

Shropshire Star.

"MR NEGASTE'S STORY has been a tissue of lies from start to finish," Martin Beddoe told Judge Patrick Halnan in Cambridge Crown Court. "After all, if God really did come to Cambridge, surely he would choose to live in Kings or Trinity, not the Open University."

Martin Beddoe was leading the prosecution case in the trial of Negusa Negaste (formerly Neville Laing, of Suez Road, Cambridge), accused of assault: "On August 27, Mr Negaste entered the Open University's offices in Hills Road, carrying a 5ft wooden cross and accompanied by his pet goat. Once inside, he informed the receptionist that he was God, and that he had returned to Earth. He also said that he had decided henceforth to live on the premises, and that she should inform her superiors immediately so that they could start building a shrine and worshipping him. At this point another employee, Peter Yates, tried to intervene, and a brief discussion ensued. But suddenly Mr Negaste announced that his pet goat had just told him that Mr Yates was in fact a cannibal and a murderer, and he began hitting him around the face with his cross. Mr Yates was taken to Addenbrooke's Hospital, and needed three stitches to a head wound."

Negaste, who admitted causing actual bodily harm, refused to withdraw his claim of divinity, but asked for leniency on the grounds of diminished responsibility. Sentence was adjourned, pending medical reports.

Cambridge Evening News.

● "ALL YE LISTEN, I am the rightful King of Zwak, and it is about time the government gave me a car," Patrick Cuntu told a bemused Supreme Court in Port Elizabeth.

Cuntu, who asked to be known by his full title of Jesus II Messiah Hephzi Bah Cuntu, was attempting to sue the South African government for R23m, following their refusal to recognise his divine right to rule over part of the Eastern Cape, which he has renamed Zwak. "What problem can there be? It is all written down in black and white in the Zwak constitution. I am the direct descendant of God and the government must pay me R1,500 a month. What's more, I am also entitled to a house and a car."

The claim was rejected by the court, on the grounds that the kingdom of Zwak did not actually exist. At this point, Mr Cuntu announced that the Clerk of the Court, Mr Cotto, was in fact the queen of Zwak. As he was being forcibly ejected from the building, he proclaimed that he would now refer the entire matter to the International Court.

Eastern Province Herald.

"These bishops are crooks. They are stupid dogs and we will piss in their eyes and swallow them," Mrs Cecilia Kankodo, chairman of the Christian Women's League told a Malawi conference on religion.

Two Catholic bishops, Chisendera and Chimole, were accused by several delegates of corruption, promiscuity and theft of pocket calculators. Mrs Hilda Manjamkbosi said: "Who does Chimole think he is? He has a face like chiboli, the ugly insect that lives underground. We will piss on his head — excuse me for my language, but I am very angry — yes, we will piss on his head. Women can piss too, if you didn't know that, and we will show him. We will shit on his head. Yes, we can take off our clothes and piss and shit on him. It is not our intention to be swearing like this, but we are very angry. God be praised."

As Chairman Dezde shouted "order", Manjamkbosi smashed a chair over the head of a television cameraman and screamed: "You photo me badly. May you have fish in your stomach for six hours and suffer illness of the bowels." The sitting was temporarily suspended.

When the conference eventually reconvened, it voted by a narrow margin in favour of urinating in the eyes of both bishops, while the Hon. Katola Phiri suggested that they should be invited to the conference and killed.

The Malawi Nation.

"HOLIDAYS ABROAD? Never again. We paid £1,000 and it was bloody hell from first to last. We're both absolutely disgusted."

Martin Mears and his wife Marina, who run the City Arms pub in Cardiff, were recounting the events of their disastrous trip to Los Cristianos, Tenerife. "Just before we arrived at the hotel, we learned that they had found the headless body of a Moroccan man in a suitcase in the foyer. It was puke-making — his head had been left on the beach. I said to Marina: 'This place isn't all it was cracked up to be in the brochure', and I was right because, when we arrived, it just got worse. On the second day, someone committed suicide by jumping off a fourth-floor balcony. I can't say I was all that surprised — the balconies were covered with barbed wire, the beds had two-inch thick foam mattresses, so nobody could sleep, and, when we complained that the floor was crawling with cockroaches, the porter threw a tin of insecticide at us and told us to fuck off in Spanish. Our taxi driver from the airport had used the same phrase when we refused him a tip, and he translated it for us."

An Airtours spokesman said: "We are concerned to hear that our clients were unhappy with aspects of their holiday. We will investigate their complaints."

Belfast News Letter.

■ "HERDING SHEEP has been Bob's whole life, and now he is very unhappy," Jane Sangster, the owner of the Grampian Dog Sanctuary at Forgue, told reporters. "The trouble is, he's twelve years old, arthritic, deaf, incontinent, and was half-blind when he was brought in. It's sad watching him try to herd sheep, because even the slowest flocks can outrun him.

"Some of our workers tried to comfort Bob with an inflatable sheep, but he wasn't fooled. The poor thing is pining away, and our only hope is to find some extremely slow sheep for him. If any of your readers live in a croft, with a few sheep that are getting on a bit themselves, then we'd be very pleased to hear from them."

The Scotsman.

"THIS ACT WAS typical of my father," Ismet Ayyildiz told reporters who had gathered outside the Uzunkopru district hospital, where Ismail Ayyildiz had just been pronounced dead. "He was a stubborn and ignorant man who knew nothing about medical science, and he always refused to seek professional help."

Ismet then explained how his father, a Turkish farmer from the western province of Edirne, had come to kill himself. "He was celebrating the total eradication of crop rot from a problem field, and had been drinking all day with friends. He kept complaining about toothache. They all told him to shut up and pay for a visit to the dentist, but he said he'd save the money and cure himself for nothing, by shooting out the aching tooth with his handgun. His friends tried to persuade him not to, but he said he'd done it before, and suddenly produced the gun and stuck the barrel against the tooth. As

the entire bar sung our glorious national anthem, my father shouted out 'I am all man. And I am thrifty. It will save on toothpaste after all,' and pulled the trigger. The bullet went in his mouth, out through the top of his head, and he was pronounced dead on arrival at the hospital. It's not been a happy time for me. I've just had a very big cleaning bill from the bar."

Jordan Times.

● **"SIR: I AM BRUCE C. Brenizer, and I am frankly disgusted with the sloppy and sensationalistic reporting that appears in your paper. I quite expect you to drag my name through the mud on a regular basis, that is your job, but at least get the facts right.**

"True, I was arrested and charged with five counts of first-degree intentional homicide in 1991. I was sentenced in 1993. You are also correct in suggesting that I had a record of violent crime and that I was responsible for the death of my father, his live-in girlfriend and her three children. But I was never charged with the murder of my half-brother as you reported. That is the trouble with you tabloid journalists, the facts are just not important to you.

"Yours, Bruce C. Brenizer, Mendota Mental Health Institute."

Editor's note: Mr Brenizer is correct. The five people he murdered included his half-sister, not his half-brother. He was ruled insane, and will be eligible for parole in about 24 years.

Wisconsin State Journal.

"THIS TOAD-LICKING craze is getting way out of hand," Rory Aikens of the Arizona Department of Fish and Game told a bemused news conference in Phoenix. "And people had better understand it's an offence under Arizona state law and we always prosecute."

Asked by reporters to explain why licking the Colorado River toad *(Bufo alvarius)* should be considered an illegal activity, Aikens continued: "The critters can be found all the way from the Mexican border to the Grand Canyon, and in parts of California. Their skin secretes a milky-white substance to deter predators, and that's what these filthy good-for-nothing toad-lickers are after. It's a combination of dimenthyltryptamine and bufotenine, which is classified as a psycho-active drug under Arizona law, and some people are hooked on licking it off the toads, or else drying the stuff and smoking it.

"We had a toad-licker jump off a building last week. He thought he could fly. I went down to the hospital and I asked him 'If you thought you could fly, why didn't you take off from ground level?' They can never answer that one. He's dead now. Kids, say no to toads." *USA Today.*

● **"I'M TELLING YOU IT'S TRUE. The facts of this matter are simple," Dr Huang Si-ming announced to reporters at Hong Kong's University of Science and Technology. "The US Government has secretly implanted a device in my teeth to control my mind, and that is why I am filing a writ against them for $100,000,000."**

Dr Huang went on to explain the circumstances that gave rise to his claim. "While undergoing root canal work at the University of Iowa in 1991, the device was secretly implanted in my teeth by a CIA dentist, so the government could trace me and find out if I was involved in criminal activity. It caused me to lose my memory, and I was sacked from my lecturing job. The device can read my thoughts and damage my career, and the mind controllers talks to my mind when I am asleep. It also acts like a video camera, sending pictures of what I see to a receiver for recording. In fact, I suspect there are two mind controllers in my teeth.

"It can also manipulate my thoughts and provoke bad behaviour like murder or visiting a prostitute. I now have bad breath and possibly foot-rot. If I am offered my job back at the university, I would be prepared to withdraw my writ. Thank you." *South China Morning Post.*

"THE VICE-PRESIDENT'S grasp of English puts Dan 'Potatoe' Quayle in the shade," Reli German told guests at a book launch in Manilla. "Only last week, when a waitress in a restaurant ignored his beckoning gestures and failed to take his order promptly, he complained to the manager with the words, 'Sir, I have been fingering your waitress for a long time, but she just does not want to come'."

The mangled syntax of Joseph "Erap" Estrada, Vice-President of the Philippines, is so famous throughout the islands that German had decided to publish a book, "ERAPtions: How To Speak English Without Really Trial". "Erap's first language is Tagalog, and whenever he speaks English he's a linguistic time bomb. For instance, during the last election campaign a TV interviewer said to him, 'I understand that when you were young you were asthmatic', and received the angry denial, 'I beg your pardon, I've always been Catholic'.

"The strange thing is, the more he does it, the more popular he gets. He used to get angry when he was ridiculed by the press, but as he himself once said: 'To avoid all that, I'll stop speaking English. From now on, I'll just speak in the binocular'."

The Australian.

■ **"I AM DISGUSTED. I feel sullied," social worker Pat Armitage told a meeting of the Adelaide Health Authority. "Frankly, I couldn't look that man in the face again."**

Mrs Armitage explained what had happened after she was asked to supervise an elderly man's personal hygiene regimen. "I called at his house, and told him I was there to help him shave and shower. At first he seemed surprised, and only let me shave him, so I used to do his dishes while he showered, but after a few days he started asking me to supervise him. I washed him all over, down the front and round the back. He said he liked to keep scrupulously clean, and insisted I was very thorough and rubbed hard with the sponge.

"Two months later, a colleague asked me how I was coping with my patient's beard, which was prone to become encrusted with dried phlegm. The chap I cleaned was not bearded, and I suddenly realised I'd been looking after the wrong man all this time. I knew there was something funny about him from the kick-off. My one lived three doors away." *The West Australian.*

"I FIRST BECAME suspicious when long queues began forming outside the Singing Sun restaurant hours before it opened," public health official Huang Shu-min told a Beijing district court. "And when the investigators we had sent there began joining the queue themselves on their days off, I knew the time had come for me to take swift action."

Huang Shu-min continued: "His squid with oyster sauce was the worst I have eaten in 37 years of public service, and yet I found myself booking lunch there every day for a fortnight." Another witness, Li Hao, concurred: "His donkey was tough, his sauces greasy, and I always left the Singing Sun telling them their food tasted like dog's dirt. Yet somehow I always went back next day."

Interrogated by health officials, Chen Tai-si, proprietor of the restaurant, eventually broke down and confessed how he managed to boost trade. "After somebody threw their dinner through the window, I decided to begin adding my special seasoning to every dish. Soon the customers were pouring in and begging for more."

Under analysis, the "special seasoning" turned out to be pure opium paste. Asking the court for leniency, Chen Tai-si declared: "They do such things as a matter of course in the West. I got the idea from a chef called Mrs Beeton. I was doing my countrymen a service. I am an innovator, not a criminal." He was sentenced to 23 years in prison for opium distribution.

Weekly World News.

"SIR: ABOUT FIVE years ago, I purchased a Redtailed Catfish. At the time, they seemed to be a popular fish at many aquatic stores. After doing hardly any research into their requirements, I chose Ragley, a five-inch fish who I thought would be ideal for my five foot tank. I soon discovered that this fish had an incredible rate of growth, and within eight months the tank was clearly too small so, after some considerable expense, a larger tank and stand were made. He lived very happily in this tank for one year before it, too, was too small. Luckily, I managed to obtain a disused 72x24x24 inch 'wave tank' from my local university, a bargain at £40.

"Today, just one year on, Ragley has undergone his latest move after outgrowing his tank. This time, however, there was a problem: there was no physical space in the house for a bigger tank. As he was now a member of the family, I did not want to sell him, so there was only one solution, and after the demolition of the garage and six months work, Ragley now lives in a 600 gallon 'tropical' pond with possibility for extensions as he grows. Friends and neighbours think I'm insane, but seeing him happily swimming in his pool with his teeth smiling all the time is all the proof I need. I would like this letter to be used as a warning to your readers. Yours sincerely, Mr Grimley, Coventry."
Aquarist and Pondkeeper.

■ **"THIS IS ALL A GREAT mystery to me," said Inspector Zitaguru to reporters, as he surveyed the carnage in a Rusape farmyard. "Tell me, why on earth would an old man, with only chickens for company, want to take a sexual stimulant?"**

Zitaguru had been called to the farm by neighbours after they discovered the body of Joseph Chatambudza, a 74-year-old who lived alone there with his poultry. "It seems that this foolish old man had unwisely swallowed a large amount of mudanhatsindi, a powerful aphrodisiac known to be lethal in high doses. We found an empty 250ml bottle, enough for twelve men, lying next to him in the yard. He must have had a seizure here, vomited prodigiously, and died, surrounded by his cockerel and thirteen hens. The unfortunate birds ate his spew and, within moments, all fourteen were dead.

"Poor Mr Chatambudza. He thought mudanhatsindi would make him as erect as the uppermost branch of a yatza tree. But now he is dead, and his cock will evermore be limp. And so shall his hens."
The Manica Post.

"I KNOW THAT, strictly speaking, you're not supposed to park on a zebra crossing," Ronald Moore told Hastings magistrates, "but I can explain everything. It would never have happened if I hadn't run myself over in my own car the previous day."

Moore, 67, of Winceby Close, Bexhill-on-Sea, explained the circumstances leading up to the offence: "My automatic garage doors wouldn't open, so I got out of the car to open them manually. My artificial leg became stuck in a drain grating and, unfortunately, I'd forgotten to put the hand brake on, and the car began rolling towards me. I was knocked over, fell under the car, my artificial leg came off and was crushed, and my good leg was trapped under the offside front wheel. I began singing loudly to attract attention, but it was several hours before I was rescued.

"Next day, I could hardly walk because my good leg was bruised, and my artificial leg was all bent into a U shape. The leg repair shop is in the centre of town, and that's why I parked on the zebra crossing. I've got arthritis and I fought in the war, you know." Mr Moore was given an absolute discharge.

Bexhill-on-Sea Observer

■ **"IT IS NOT OUR WISH that the garage be punished. It is God's," said Malcolm Heap, founder of the Fundamentalist Christian group "Midnight Ministries".**

Heap went berserk after a BMW garage in Aylesbury refused to give him a £22,000 car for free. "God spoke to my son Richard, saying that we would receive the gift of a red 325i BMW estate car to do His work. So I wrote to the garage, telling them the ins and outs and advising them to get the car ready. We even bought spare parts for the 325i in advance. God had told us to buy a little cap to go on top of the windscreen wiper bottle, and some oil and a filter, because we would need them. But, when we went to collect the car, the sales staff just laughed at us. It was blasphemy."

"The Lord Himself told us that the garage must close," said Heap, who immediately wrote to BMW: "Keep this letter, because when you're standing in the dole queue looking for another job, it will help you to realise exactly how much God is in charge of everything."

At that point, the garage manager decided to refer the entire matter to the police. *Bucks Herald.*

"IT IS TRUE, OUR priest is not human," Zen Buddhist monk Hirata Isao admitted to reporters in the Yokohama Central Cemetery, "but let us dwell on the positive side. He never turns up to services drunk, he does not touch the young boys and, in all, he is completely moral and trustworthy."

The reporters had gathered to watch *Robopriest*, a fully-ordained robot cleric who has been saying prayers in the cemetery since 1992. Isao (his inventor) continued: "He is well-versed in the liturgy of ten Japanese Buddhist sects and, when he chants the sutras, his lips and facial muscles move in time to the prerecorded blessings. He also bows his head and closes his eyes, in the manner prescribed in ancient scriptures. Most real human priests are not half as diligent as him. They turn up late, rush through the morning service, leaving half of it out, then drive off to play golf. But not *Robopriest*.

"Drawbacks? Only one. He is not fully waterproof and, when we have heavy rain, he speaks garbled rubbish or repeats himself. One service lasted four days. In the end, we had to unplug him."

Toronto Globe & Mail.

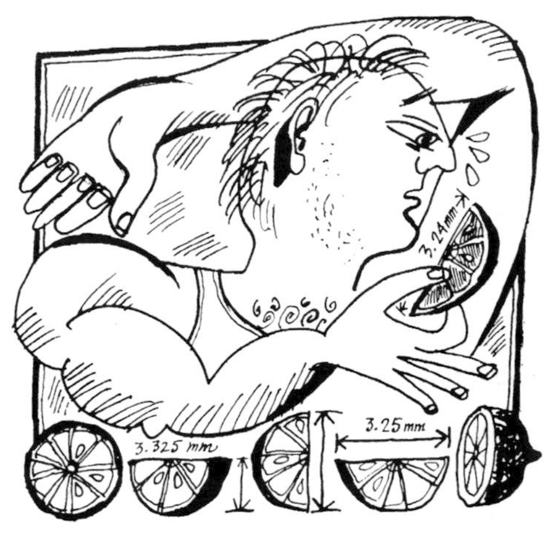

● *"DEAR SIR: Has anyone else noticed that the acidity of the Valencian Lemon is on the wane?*

"As always, I slice my lemons at intervals of 2.75mm and, up to this month, two slices added to my 20ml of gin and 20ml of tonic always had the desired effect. Now, however, I fear the two slices lack their normal efficaciousness.

"Why is this happening? I blame the ozone layer. Until I receive definite proof of the cause I have decided, in the interests of science, to up the gin content to see if that does the trick. My wife says I should start cutting my lemon slightly thicker, or put three slices in, but why should I change the habits of a lifetime, just because deodorant is being squirted under someone's armpit?

"Yours sincerely, Arnold Bolton."

Costa Blanca News.

● **"AT THE TIME, it seemed like a miracle," Brenda Murphy told the vicar of St John with St Michael, Bournemouth.**

"Two weeks ago, I was having a picnic on the lawn and my little daughter said she wanted a cat. I told her to ask Jesus for one, so she started to pray. Barely ten seconds later, this pussy suddenly came hurtling through the air, screeching very loudly, and landed inside our wicker hamper. It's stayed with us ever since. What was I to think?"

While reclaiming his cat, the vicar was able to offer a more prosaic explanation of events to astonished parishioners. "Two weeks ago, Horace became stuck in a tree. I couldn't get him down, so I climbed up as far as I could, tied one end of a rope around the trunk, and the other to my car bumper. Then I drove slowly forward, bending the bough nearer to the ground. Unfortunately my foot slipped on the accelerator, the car shot forward, the rope broke, and Horace was catapulted into space and clean out of sight. There was no sign of him at all. If I hadn't seen Brenda buying cat food in Tesco's, when I knew she didn't have a cat, Horace's whereabouts would still be a puzzle. The Lord moves in mysterious ways indeed. Praise Him."

Bournemouth Advertiser.

"MY TOUR OF Guyana was proceeding without a hitch until we reached Lethem," said Philip Barton, a British volunteer dentist working in South America.

"I got out of the truck to relieve myself by the roadside, and was promptly stung on the end of my winkle by a large jungle wasp. I jumped onto the back of the truck and curled up in such immense pain that I failed to spot the razor grass overhanging the road. Before I knew it the grass had cut through my skin like a knife through butter, leaving me raw and bleeding. By now, pretty annoyed, I leant back against the fuel tank and straight onto a scorpion, which stung me twice in the back. Seeking revenge, I grabbed at the insect, and got stung again on the fingers. I learnt a lot about pain in those few hours. Still, I thoroughly enjoyed the trip."

Dental Practice.

"YOU DON'T THINK of a Morphy Richards hair dryer as a dangerous weapon," said a spokesman for the Ilkeston police, "but the way Howard Tyler used it, it could have caused serious injury."

31 year-old Tyler, unemployed, had earlier received his sixth official warning for impersonating a traffic policeman. "He was angry with motorists driving at eighty past his house," the spokesman explained, "so he started dressing up in a dark suit and peaked cap, and stood on the pavement with his wife's hair dryer, pointing it at approaching cars. Drivers naturally thought it was a radar gun and slammed on their brakes. We had skid marks a hundred yards long up the road." Speaking outside his house, Tyler condemned police conduct. "If a man isn't free to use his own domestic appliances in the open air, then I call it fascism. Anyway, I'm doing their job for them, they ought to pay me. Including time and a half for weekends."

Derby Evening Telegraph.

■ *"LET'S GET ONE thing very clear. Wank Associates Inc is a world leader in the field of public relations and literary criticism," President Martin Wank declared in a press statement.*

"There is nothing remotely funny about the name. There are Wanks everywhere. On Long Island alone, there are more than a dozen distinguished Wanks. The Pennsylvanian printing firm founded by my father, Joseph Wank, still bears his name, and there are many more in Texas. It's Bavarian in origin, you know. There is a mountain called Wank, and the village of Wank stands nearby. Have you never heard of the river Wankova near the Polish border? Have you never tasted Wank potato chips? Never had a Wank cocktail? I'm telling you, it's a perfectly normal name."

When Mr Wank was informed that neither the mountain, river, nor village were listed in a major world atlas — nor had anybody heard of the potato chip or cocktail — he said: "Wank is not penetrating the British market. That is the problem."

■ "THIS SITUATION HAS got completely out of control," Mike and Barbara Holder told astonished reporters at their home near Cinderford in the Forest of Dean. "The curry poisoner is trying to kill us, yet the police do nothing. We need help."

The Holders were speaking after being discharged from Gloucestershire Royal Hospital, where they had both complained of severe sickness after eating home-made turkey curry. "It all began last October, when the poisoner began preying on our animals. Several cats were killed, a goose was poisoned, one of our goats became violently ill, and two pet cockatiels died in mysterious circumstances which have never been satisfactorily explained. That was when we decided to install the security cameras."

Mr Holder then explained what had happened earlier that evening. "Obviously, the poisoner must have broken into our kitchen and put drugs into our curry. I began hallucinating soon after dinner, and was convinced that my wife was turning into a roll of Sellotape and that my nose and eyebrows were growing longer and my teeth were igniting. I felt I was disappearing, floating up. But I am certain that we now have the curry poisoner on film. The video shows him coming to the gate, at which point we lose sight of him. Three minutes elapse. He must have got in through a window and put something in the fridge where the curry was. Somebody is trying to kill us. It's the only explanation."

A police spokesman said later: "The couple have presented evidence to us, but we do not intend taking any further action".

Western Daily Express.

■ "UNTIL A MONTH ago, Heidi Pork Tenderloin was Oink-Oink Inc's best-selling product," said R. Miles Handy, president of the Detroit corporation. "They're made from the penises of male hogs, and dogs love 'em. I got the idea of making pig penises into pet treats around the time of the Lorena Bobbitt trial. We were already using pig ears, hoofs, snouts, hearts, feet and liver. So why not the pizzles? Then it really would be everything but the squeak.

"Things went fine until last month, when an inspector from the agriculture department told us we'd have to dye them green, 'denaturing' them to show they're not fit for human consumption. But most dogs won't eat 'em if they're green, so we've stopped making them. We're losing $100,000 a month in sales, and dog owners are going crazy because we're out of this product.

"My Congressman, Rep. Joe Knollenberg, is trying to get this whole green penis issue overturned. It's ridiculous. Like all Oinkers' products, Heidi Pork Tenderloin is clean and wholesome. You could feed it to your kids. At this rate, I'm gonna have to start importing foreign pig pizzles, just to meet demand. And who wants a foreign pig penis in their mouths? Don't answer that."

The Detroit Herald.

"ALRIGHT, I KNOW Christians are supposed to turn the other cheek, but no way. I'm Hanger by name and Hanger by nature. Give me the rope and I'll string her up myself."

Sister Marie Hanger, an education coordinator for the Catholic Church, lashed out at Susan Butler, publisher of the Macquarie Thesaurus, during Melbourne TV's "Right to Gripe". "This book is a reflection of our sick society," she screamed, "full of vile similes including 'as dry as a nun's cunt' and 'as cold as a nun's tits'. Just what sort of language is that?" The programme was taken off air before Ms Butler could answer.

In a statement released the next day to the press, Ms Butler said: "It is not a dictionary's role to act as language police, or to stop people from using offensive words. The nun was quoting from our book, so at least she found it useful. We've had no letters from the gay community objecting to expressions like 'fudge-packers' or 'turd burglars'. Anyway, she's no Missy Innocent herself. Before the show started, one of the cameraman broke wind and she shouted out 'Who cut the cheese?' That expression, incidentally, appears on page 436 of the thesaurus. 22 dollars. Available at all good bookshops."

Australian Times.

Q: "I often turn to your excellent problem page in the Arab News, but never thought I would one day require its services. I am suffering because my ablution is frequently invalidated as a result of wind. I am often unable to complete my prayer with the same ablution, and have to leave the mosque to have a fresh ablution. I also fear I may dim candles..."

Problem page in Arab News.

"THERE WAS A MASSIVE explosion and what looked like a bomb came crashing through my roof," George Neseveremko told reporters from his house in Thornhill, north of Toronto. "It landed right by the bed, missing us by about two feet, and it smelt very, very bad."

Neseveremko's wife, Fanzia Zaig, continued the story: "When we turned the lights on and looked at it, we saw it was a huge block of ice, with hundreds of lumps of crap in it. There were sheets of used toilet paper and old tampons too. I tried to phone the police, but they couldn't understand me because I kept retching. When they turned up, they put gas masks on, so we couldn't understand what they were saying, and they just left. A government official arrived and told us it must have fallen out of an airplane's on-board toilet and it was our responsibility to move it, but it's far too heavy for us to lift, so it's been slowly melting in our bedroom for the past two days. The stench is making us sick."

Bruce Reid, spokesperson for Pearson International Airport, played down the entire incident. "The tanks can only hold so much, then they have to be emptied," he said, "and at high altitudes the liquid sometimes freezes solid. There's no panic though. We only have an incident like this every month or so."

London Free Press [Ontario].

"MY CLIENT HAS BEEN getting sexual stimulation by watching women in this way for many years, without previously causing any offence," Adrian Cole told magistrates in a Salisbury court. "Indeed, if his metal coat hanger had not become ensnared in a bramble bush this time, no one would have been inconvenienced in any way."

Mr Cole was defending John Ulicsny, 35, of Estcourt Road, Salisbury, who was in court on a charge of indecent behaviour. "As a teenager, my client was keen on collecting butterflies, but this innocent hobby soon led him to start hiding behind hedges, spying on women as they walk along the footpath. He always removes his clothing first, wraps a butterfly-type metal coat hanger around his waist, and tightens two neck ties round the top of his legs to increase arousal.

"Unfortunately, on this occasion, the hanger snagged on some brambles, and he fell headlong into a bush, covering himself in deep and painful scratches. In extricating himself, he stumbled out in front of a woman walking her dog, panicked when he realised he'd been seen, and tried to hide himself by diving back into the bushes. That was where the police picked him up. He is now receiving psychiatric help, and deserves pity rather than punishment."

Ulicsny was given 12 months' probation. Magistrates ordered the destruction of the ties and the coat hanger. *Salisbury Journal.*

"Toughness contests are a traditional part of Polish recreational life," Regional Prosecutor Stefan Wojcelski told a court in Stargard Szczeciski, "and the state has no wish to interfere with a playful tradition. But, while we accept amputation as an inevitable part of this, we do not accept the murder, and I therefore ask for the heaviest penalties to be brought against the three accused.

Wojcelski, who was leading the prosecution of three men accused of manslaughter, explained what had happened. "The three men had been drinking solidly all Sunday in the garden of Krzysztof Azninski, the dead man. They put on traditional toughness bonnets and began a contest. At first they played breath holding contests. Then they hit each other with blocks of wood and banged nails into their own flesh. But then Franciszek Zyzcoszusko put his hand on a chopping block, and dared Krzysztof A to cut it off. Krzysztof A hacked at it with a knife, partially severing the wrist, then put his own head on the block and challenged Franciszek Z to chop it off.

Franciszek Z beheaded him with an axe, then the three men decided things had gone too far, stopped the contest, and began singing a folksong called 'Roll the head of the giant', which woke the neighbours. That's when they were observed burying the body in the garden."

The three accused pleaded not guilty, on grounds of drunkenness.

Polish News Agency.

"WE ARE A PROUD parish, and we are proud of our name," Dr Hugh O'Neill warned Cork County Council at a public meeting in the Bride Valley, "which is why we object so strongly to this proposal. Apart from the environmental concerns, if Munster Crematorium Ltd are allowed to build their factory here, then Ovens will become nothing more than the butt of crematorium jokes."

Dr O'Neill was leading a delegation of 400 residents from Ovens, Co. Cork, who had signed a petition (organised by the Ovens Community Group) against the siting of Munster's first crematorium in their parish: "Already, graffiti is appearing on walls saying 'Ovens — the crem de la crem'. If building goes ahead, generations to come will think the place was called Ovens because of the crematorium. Humorous postcards will be printed. What is more, the livelihood of fruit farmers would suffer." *The Irish Times.*

■ **GIVE US NON-CANCER packs... we want non-cancer packs now!" shouted a group of protesting farm workers outside a tobacconist's in Eastern Cape. Their spokesman, Hiddi Marhubi, told news reporters: "We will not buy a packet that says *'Danger: Smoking Can Kill You'*. Give us safe packets now."**

A South African television reporter later confirmed that scenes like these have become common throughout the Eastern Cape in recent weeks, since the government decided to adopt statutory health warnings on all cigarette packets. "The irate farm workers are demanding the return of the unmarked packs that they used to be able to buy before the health warnings were added, because they think those weren't lethal. Tobacconists report that these workers absolutely refuse to buy the new packs with *'Smoking Causes Cancer'* or *'The More You Smoke, The Sooner You'll Die'* printed on them. Even sales of packets reading *'Smoking Can Cause Low Birth Weight'* have plummeted, although some of the men are prepared to risk smoking those packs." *Business Day [Johannesburg].*

"IT WAS THE WORST DAY of my life," Lonnie Hensley told a jury in Charleston, West Virginia. "One minute we were joking how she'd be better than Dolly Parton. Next I was covered in blood and standing with nothing but the waistband of my pants on."

Lonnie was giving evidence at the trial of Denny Ray Gullett, who was accused of murdering his business partner, Masel Hensley, in order to collect $250,000 life insurance. "Denny called me into his office and asked me to give a box to Masel. He said it was 'an inflatable doll with Dolly Parton's body and Ronald Reagan's head' and promised Masel would 'get a real bang out of it'. I took it to Masel, who was a big Dolly Parton fan, and we thought we'd fuck it there and then. The instructions on the box told us to hook the wires up to a car battery so it could inflate, and we were joking about who'd go first while he fixed it to his pick-up truck. Then everything just blowed up."

A forensic expert later testified that the box had not contained an inflatable sex doll. It had, in fact, contained six sticks of dynamite powerful enough to crack the foundations of a nearby house and rip the clothes from both men, depositing the remnants on power lines overhead. Masel was killed outright by the explosion, Lonnie had his testicles blown off and was later found wandering the streets singing "Stand By Your Man" in a daze. He now walks with a limp. Gullett's defence — that the gift wrapping department of his local store had "obviously screwed up and given me the wrong package" — was not accepted by the jury.

New Haven Register.

"BARRY BRINKSMAN is an ingenious but evil man," prosecutor Steven Ipsen told a Los Angeles court. "He claimed to be an alien being, recruiting for a utopian, matriarchal planet in a distant galaxy, when he was in fact a fat, bald, one-armed bespectacled pervert, living in the Tropicana Hotel in Las Vegas and seducing adolescent girls."

Ipsen outlined how Brinksman, 59, had committed numerous sexual offences during the summer of 1990: "He told the girls that he came from Cablell, an all-Caucasian planet ruled by a Queen Click-Clack, and that his spaceship was parked at Lake Tahoe, not far from San Francisco. He said that on Cablell everyone lived by free will, and that sexual intercourse was mental, not physical. But, before they could visit his planet, the girls first had to lower their subconscious intelligence barriers, so they would be less concerned with earthly morality. and they could only do this by drinking Cablellian Ambrosia (Chivas Regal served from Tupperware mugs) and playing strip poker with him. He also told the girls that the other problem about travelling to Cablell was that they could get diseases from intergalactic space travel. The only way to build up their immunity was to have sex with him, so they could receive IREs the antibodies needed to counter the diseases. They had to have an IRE level of 100 before they could travel through space and that would take months of sex."

The trial ended with Brinksman receiving a 20-year jail sentence. One of his victims, now aged 18, admitted afterwards: "I don't feel like I was the smartest of people for going along with it." *South China Morning Post.*

"LAST THURSDAY morning, while driving along Shaikh Salman Highway, I saw two men throwing live kittens out of the window of their van into the path of oncoming traffic. Worse, they cheered whenever one became squashed beneath those of the oncoming wheels. Such men should be pushed away with water and broom even to the bottom of the sea.

"I was most alarmed to see such an inhumane way of disposing rid of unwanted pets, and urge all readers to show greater thoughtfulness by drowning them painlessly in a bucket.

"Yours, a shocked animal lover."

Gulf Daily News.

● "DEAR AUNT LAI SU; I write to your esteemed problem page in the hope that you can help me and my wife with our difficulty. Life for us has always been a bit of a struggle., because we have three children, but it is made a bit easier because my wife works in a meat processing factory. We really need the money it brings in. My problem is that even though she is a clean woman and regularly showers, whenever she makes love, as she heats up, I can smell roast pork coming out of her body. I do not like the smell of meat as I enjoy penetration and I would really like her to change her job, but she says that jobs are not easy to get. Is there a solution?"

Agony Aunt Lai Su replied: "Stuff two wads of cotton wool up your nostrils before sex, and be grateful she does not work in a fish factory. Some men write to me about such a problem when their wives do not even work at fish factories." *The Foreign Post [Philippines].*

"DO WE STINK? Are we dirty? Give us money or we will smash all your flower pots, even the big ones," enraged eunuchs screamed at a Delhi housewife.

For months the residents of Chittranjan Park, South Delhi, have been terrorised by a gang of belligerent eunuchs, who burst into newly constructed houses and demand money from the owners, threatening to damage their property if they refuse. "I pleaded with them that our house was still incomplete," the tearful wife of an army officer told reporters, "but they said they were incomplete too and kept chanting 'Our purses are long and empty like the pumpkins of a man from Salli — pay up' and demanded 1,100 rupees." When Mr P.R. Bhattacharya refused to pay them 2,001 rupees they stripped naked and assaulted his relatives by breaking wind in their faces. "I was in the middle of performing grih puja at the time, and had to hide in the bathroom," he complained to police. Dozens of similar cases have been reported.

A spokesman for the East Pakistan Displaced Persons' Association complained that the authorities were turning a blind eye to the eunuchs' behaviour: "You can't catch them anyway. Those without testicles can run like the wind."

The Times of India News.

"LET ME TELL YOU a few home truths about my opponent," Lighton Ndefwayl, the Medjian closed tennis champion, told reporters after unexpectedly losing in a two hour match.

"Musumba Bwayla is a man who farts when he walks, and he is a hopeless player. He has a huge nose, several warts, and he is cross-eyed. Girls hate him, and women laugh at him. The reason he beat me is obvious. My jockstrap was too tight so that, whenever I tried to perform my legendary overarm smash, my eyes watered and I could no longer see the ball. Also, when Bwayla walks, he farts very loudly. He does it when he serves too, and that made me lose my concentration for which I am famous through Zambia. They do not allow such things at Wimbledon. The umpire has failed me. Official protests will follow."

The Star Tonight.

■ **"THE government must crack down on this disgusting craze of 'Pumping'," a spokesman for the Nakhon Ratchasima hospital told reporters. "If this perversion catches on, it will destroy the cream of Thailand's manhood."**

He was speaking after the remains of 13 year-old Charnchai Puanmuangpak had been brought into the hospital's emergency department. "Most Pumpers use a standard bicycle pump," he explained, "sticking the nozzle up their rectum and giving themselves a rush of air. Not only is that a sin against God, but it can be dangerous even for onlookers. Charnchai took it further still. He started using a two-cylinder foot pump, but even that wasn't exciting enough for him, and he boasted to friends that he was going to try the compressed air hose at a nearby gasoline station. They dared him to do it so, under cover of darkness, he sneaked in. Not realising how powerful the machine was, he inserted the tube into his body, and placed a 1 baht coin in the slot. Of course, he died instantly, but passers-by are still in shock. One woman thought she was watching a twilight firework display and started clapping. We still haven't located all of him.

"Pumping is the devil's pastime, and we must all say no to Satan," he concluded. "Inflate your tyres by all means, but then hide your bicycle pump where it cannot tempt you."

The Japan Times.

"WE ARE BITTERLY disappointed and disgusted by this late cancellation," an angry Rolando Navarro told Filipino reporters. "The crucifixion is traditionally the highlight of our Good Friday celebrations. I only hope there is still time to find a suitable replacement for this thoughtless, irresponsible man."

Speaking in the farming village of San Pedro Cutud, north of Manila, festival organiser Navarro explained what had happened. "For centuries, we have crucified a Filipino man or woman each year, as part of our Easter rites. It is a great honour to be chosen, and locals vie for the chance to be nailed to the cross in imitation of our Lord. But a few years ago, a Belgian nun called Godelieve Rombaut asked us to crucify her instead, so we did. It was a great success, and this year when another Belgian, Roland Brauwers, said that he wanted to be crucified too we were happy to allow him to re-enact the passion of Jesus Christ our saviour.

"But this morning, only days before the ceremony is due to begin, I received this letter from him, saying he regrets that he cannot take part 'due to a heavy head cold, which could be a problem on the cross, what with not having access to hankies or the like,' but that he hopes to be alright to be crucified next year. I phoned his hotel in Manila and they said he had departed hurriedly at the weekend after emptying the contents of the minibar into his briefcase, and without paying his bill. I tell you, if he comes here next year expecting us to crucify him, we'll bloody lynch him. Typical Belgian."

China News.

"I DO NOT BLAME the congregation for their actions," declared Mhlengi Ginindz from his hospital bed in Manzini. "They were only carrying out the Lord's will. I blame the brewery — there was too much yeast in the beer."

Ginindz told reporters how he had sustained his injuries at an all-night peace vigil: "After some beers in the sheeben, I entered the church and took my rightful place in the pew. But the beer was very bad, and it wreaked havoc inside my stomach, so I moved to the back of the church and, holding my cheeks apart so as not to cause offence, began farting quietly. I became drowsy and fell asleep, and the next thing I knew I was hanging upside down from a 'Jesus Our Saviour' banner, being bludgeoned by hysterical members of the Red Gown Zionist Sect. They said I had been farting during the lesson, and began hitting me with a large wooden cross. The priest then denounced me from the pulpit, saying that the devil must have sent me to drown out the word of God, because my farting was louder than the rumble of thunder. He told the congregation to drive Satan from his church, so they beat me with crucifixes, fractured my pelvis, broke both my legs, and rammed communion wafers up my nose with crayons from the Sunday school activity box. If I had not crawled outside and sheltered beneath the protective branches of an umhlanga tree, it could have been serious.

"And now they are claiming I was hit by a milk truck. Where is the truck? It is a lie. However, I will not prosecute. They are very devout in Manzini."

The Times of Swaziland.

● "YOU'RE GUILTY, I'm certain of that, but I simply can't bear to listen to your damned accountant any longer," announced a tearful Judge Sandra Hamilton to an almost deserted Alberta court.

Hamilton, who was presiding over a case involving the Del Fisher insurance company on 15 counts of tax evasion, continued: "It is my observation that your accountant, Ernie Bretz, is beyond a doubt the dullest witness I've ever had in my court. He speaks in a monotonal voice so totally devoid of interest, and uses language so drab and convoluted, that even the court reporter cannot stay conscious long enough to record his evidence properly. I've had it. Three solid days of his steady drone as he defends an obviously fraudulent set of end-of-year accounts is enough. I cannot face the prospect of another 14 indictments. It's probably unethical, but I don't care. Case dismissed."
International Accountancy Bulletin.

A GHANAIAN coroner's court has heard from a friend of the late Theophilus Kwarme Gakpo how he became impatient while he waited in a long queue outside a public convenience in Accra. "He insisted we should use the manhole behind the main toilet instead, even though it meant trespassing. We climbed the fence, prised off the slabs, and then he squatted at the edge to relieve himself. His last words to me were: 'I must have eaten well last night, a flock of sparrows is leaving me'. Unfortunately the rain had made the slabs slippery and Theophilus slipped to his death. His grandmother always said he would end up in deep shit."

The coroner recorded a verdict of death by misadventure.
The Nation [Indonesia].

"I don't like doing this," Judge David Leahy told defendant Kenneth Saasta while pronouncing sentence, "because cocaine dealing carries a mandatory prison sentence. But, after looking at all the evidence, I'm gonna have to let you off with community service, because you're so goddam fat you'd break the jail."

Saasta, who had earlier pleaded guilty in the Santa Clara Superior Court to the possession and sale of narcotics, grinned as prosecuting attorney Cynthia Sevely begged the judge not to impose a custodial sentence: "Saasta weights more than 650 pounds (approx. 47 stone), and there isn't a jail in the state that can hold him. We have to prise him in through the cell doors. The night he was arrested, he demolished all the bunks in the police cells by lying down on them, and smashed three toilets simply by sitting on them. No prison uniforms will fit him, he can't stand for more than 5 minutes but chairs collapse when he sits on them, and because of this problem with constant diarrhoea, we have to hose everywhere he's been. Even, as you can see, this court room... The jail would need to buy reinforced beds, chairs and toilets, and worse, he's so fat he can't even cut his own toenails or wipe himself in the bathroom. Someone has to do it for him, and the sheriff's department is threatening strike action if Saasta is sent to jail."

Judge Leahy also ordered that Saasta be tagged with an electronic monitoring device, but this ruling was overturned when it was discovered that none of the devices was large enough to fit round his ankle.

San Jose Mercury News.

■ "THANK GOD THAT I am still alive after all these accidents," Muhammad Areeshi told reporters in Jeddah after he had been dragged unharmed from the ruins of his twenty-fifth serious road crash. "In truth, I am surprised to have survived so long. I praise Allah for his generosity in keeping me alive. He is great."

Areeshi, who has been driving in and around the city of Jizan for the past two years, has so far spent a total of SR236,000 on 22 cars, all of which he has subsequently wrecked. "My friends are afraid to travel with me, because I have accidents so frequently. But they are wrong to be nervous because it is always the people in the other cars who die or are injured, never me. I now wear a permanent neck brace, so naturally it is difficult turning corners as I can only see straight ahead, but I give hooter warnings. Most of my accidents occur along the Taif-Riyadh road. I've written off a 1977 model Jeep there, two Cressidas, a Land Rover, a Chevette, and a Hilux pickup. That accident killed all the cows I had on board, but I survived. And the cows were evil. Their nose steam temporarily blinded me. I am in pain, however. I still have my sense of humour and, when people call me a reckless driver I laugh and tell them they are wrong, because I have already sold 22 wrecks to the Jizan scrapyard.

"No, I do not bother with insurance. I believe in fate and trust in Allah."
Arab News.

"ELK ARE A VERY serious traffic problem in this country," Torsten Lumabba of the Finnish Transport Ministry told a press conference in Helsinki. "There are lots of them, they're very big, they're not very clever, and they don't take any notice of road signs."

The conference had been called to draw attention to the threat posed to Finnish motorists by wandering elk, the country's biggest non-alcoholic cause of road accidents. "There are hundreds of collisions every year, and up to a dozen Finns die annually after elk-related incidents," Lumabba continued. "Finland is still mourning the loss of its most celebrated tango singer, the legendary Sauli Lehtonen, after a fatal encounter with a full-grown elk earlier this month. The problem is they have rather spindly legs. You hit them with a car and they sort of flip onto the roof and crush you. Or you drive into a tree trying to avoid them.

"The government is spending £15 million on building elk underpasses. They'll be 30ft wide and 20ft high so the elk can see the other side. They have to be huge, because there's no way you'll get one of them into a tunnel. Not an elk."
Associated Press.

"I ATE DOG FOOD because people often dismiss the resurrection of Jesus," church minister Donna Dobson explained to bemused worshippers, after she had finished preaching her Sunday sermon in Chipping Sodbury Baptist Church. "They want proof that he came back to life, and that's why I ate the Chum.

"You see, people didn't believe they would ever see a minister eat a tin of dog food in church," continued Ms Dobson, 35, who lives alone with her dog Sally, "so I did it before their eyes to provide the proof. I chose a can of chicken-flavoured Pedigree Chum, the one top breeders recommend, and I blessed it before smothering it in tomato sauce and tucking in. The congregation reacted very well to it all, and it certainly made them take notice. Pedigree Chum tastes all right, and I was pleasantly surprised. When I was little, I was not allowed tea by my parents if I'd been naughty, so I often used to eat dog food, but it was not very nice back then and I can honestly say the flavour has improved."

Mike Jenkins of Pedigree Dog Foods said: "All our products are perfectly safe if people decide to eat them."
Bristol Evening Post.